Giving Professional Presentations
in the Behavioral Sciences
and
Related Fields

A Practical Guide for the Novice, the Nervous, and the Nonchalant

Michael J. Platow

Psychology Press
Taylor & Francis Group

NEW YORK AND HOVE

Published in 2002 by
Psychology Press, Inc.
29 West 35th Street
New York, NY 10001
www.psypress.com

Published in Great Britain by
Psychology Press, Ltd.
27 Church Road
Hove, East Sussex
BN3 2FA
www.psypress.co.uk

Psychology Press, Inc., is an imprint of the Taylor & Francis Group.
Printed in the United States of America on acid-free paper.

10 9 8 7 6 5 4 3 2 1

Library of Congress Cataloging-in-Publication Data
Platow, Michael.
    Giving professional presentations in the behavioral sciences and related fields : a
practical guide for the novice, the nervous, and the nonchalant / Michael J. Platow.
      p. cm.
    Includes bibliographical references and index.
    ISBN 1–84169–059–7 — ISBN 1–84169–060–0 (pbk.)
    1. Public speaking. 2. Communication in the social sciences. I. Title.

PN4129.15 .P53 2002
808.5'1—dc21   2002022671

Cover design: Pearl Chang

GIVING PROFESSIONAL PRESENTATIONS
IN THE BEHAVIORAL SCIENCES AND
RELATED

Contents

Acknowledgments

I owe several people my sincere thanks for their many forms of assistance in writing this book. It would not have been possible without them. The first and foremost thanks must go to all of the speakers I have seen who have given poor professional presentations. I have seen so many, and cringed so often with embarrassment for these people that I was compelled finally to write down some basic advice for them and others. I sincerely hope that if any of these people read this and recognize themselves in my examples, they will understand that I am not poking fun at them. I have, in fact, been inspired and moved to help them and those who follow. In an attempt to maintain their anonymity, I have, of course, made some changes in the descriptions. The second thanks must go to all of those outrageously impolite audience members who have given me a hard time in my own presentations. These people have allowed me to hone my presentation skills and develop successful strategies to combat their impeccable rudeness.

Thanks is owed to the School of Psychology at the Australian National University, and to the Department of Work and Organisational Psychology at the University of Amsterdam. It was at these two universities that I actually wrote this book during my sabbatical. Finally, there are, of course, specific individuals who helped me with this book by giving input at various stages. These are Simon Crowe, Geoff Cumming, Ross Day, Yoshi Kashima, Tony Love, and Joseph Platow. Elizabeth Marsh, Alison Mudditt, and one anonymous reviewer each commented on a complete draft and provided several suggestions that have greatly improved the book. And Paul Dukes, Hope Breeman, and their entire team deserve a great thanks for the fantastic work they put into bringing this book to being.

Finally, particularly great thanks is owed to Diana Grace for meticulously reading and commenting on multiple versions of this book, and for enduring any time I spent away from her and our family while writing this book. Of course, any problems, unclarities, and errors in the book remain my responsibility.

Michael J. Platow
Melbourne

Introduction

The prospect of public speaking strikes fear in many people. It may come as no surprise to you that fear of public speaking is common and, for those who suffer from it, often very intense. Despite this, many professionals will have to make public presentations in one capacity or another over the course of their careers. Sometimes they will have to present new ideas or progress reports to their colleagues and bosses, or sometimes they will share the findings of their latest clinical or scientific inquiries with their peers. The size of their audience will vary from just a couple of people to an entire lecture theater. What makes dealing with their fear even worse is that most people have never been taught how to give a professional presentation. This simple lack of knowledge compounds any existing anxiety that people already have over "looking stupid," "completely flopping," "being ripped apart by the audience," boring the audience, or simply just forgetting what they were going to say. The purpose of this book is to provide some guidance in the how-tos of giving professional presentations. The main goal is to give you practical advice on organizing and delivering your presentations. In doing so, I provide basic guidelines. Of course, not every situation you may encounter is considered in this book. You will have to use this book in a thinking, interactive manner. Some of my advice will not be suitable for some of your professional presentations. Fear not, however; most of the advice will.

As I say in the subtitle, I wrote this book with three groups of speakers in mind. The first group consists of those people who have little or no experience in giving professional presentations—the novice. This group includes students and young professionals in the early stages of their careers. Most people are, unfortunately, never provided with the instruction they need to give good professional presentations despite the great importance of presentations in many professional contexts. The second group of people I had in mind when writing this book is those who are particularly anxious about public speaking—the "nervous." Fear of public speaking is quite strong among many people, despite the necessity for it in their careers. I must be clear at this point: This is not a book outlining clinically based strategies for helping people overcome their fear of public speaking. It is, instead, a how-to book designed to provide people with enough guidance in giving professional presentations that at least some of their fears can be assuaged. Finally, the third group of people that I had in mind when writing this book is those who may have given some professional presentations in the past, but who have been rather unsuccessful because of a lack of proper preparation—the "nonchalant." Some professionals may find themselves frequently giving presentations with consistently poor results because they have not given proper attention to preparation. The advice I outline in this book should assist these people in their presentation preparation.

You will benefit most from the first three chapters of this book. These are the most important chapters, as they outline the groundwork for giving professional presentations. In the first chapter, "Design: Preparing Your Presentation," I outline practical advice on preparing presentations, from knowing your goals to choosing your overhead fonts. In the second chapter, "Delivery: Presenting Your Work," I outline practical advice on actually giving your presentation, from projecting your voice to dealing with stage fright. And in the third chapter, "Defense: Answering Questions and Defending Your Work," I give you practical advice on answering questions from your audience, from dealing with rude audience members to dealing with right audience members. You'll notice that each one of these three chapters gets progressively shorter. This should tell you something immediately. Successful presentations are ones in which presenters have spent time and worked hard *prior* to their arrival at their presentation venue. Your homework is essential. Most of your success will come in designing your presentation, and for this reason I have dedicated the most amount of space to this section. All this, of course, is assuming (as I will throughout the book) that you have something meaningful to say. Without that, no amount of preparation will make for a successful presentation.

The fourth chapter, "Persuasion: On Being More Influential," summarizes some of the lessons learned from experimental social psychology on attitude change and social influence. Note that these are finishing touches only. Following these tips without following the lessons in the preceding chapters—and without having something meaningful to say—

will not automatically make you persuasive. In fact, it may just make you look foolish. There are no shortcuts. Be warned ahead of time.

In the fifth chapter, "Pedagogy: Some Comments on Teaching," I outline some similarities between giving professional presentations and lecturing to students. There are some important differences, however, and I outline these too. Finally, the sixth chapter, "Prototypes: Examples of Good and Bad Overheads and Slides," is just that: examples. I have included these as supplements to the first three chapters.

Finally, you will also notice that I have included summary tables in chapters 1 through 5. These are to help organize your thoughts after you've read each section. Of course, if you are so inclined, you can read these tables without the preceding text. However, I have not written the book to be used that easily. The text provides important information not presented in the tables; that's why I wrote it in the first place. You will benefit the most if you read the complete text.

Chapter 1

Design
Preparing your presentation

Planning your presentation

Know your goals for your presentation

The most important thing you need to know when you write a professional presentation is why you are giving the presentation in the first place. This may sound a bit silly, as we often take the reason as self-evident. But on reflection, part of the anxiety people often feel about giving a professional presentation stems in part from not knowing exactly what they are supposed to be doing. And for this reason, they often try to put a little bit of everything into the presentation, resulting only in a muddled mess.

The wrong goals

Let's first consider two of the most common—yet wrong—goals of professional presentations: (1) demonstrating encyclopedia skills, and (2) demonstrating statistical and methodological skills.

    One reason for anxiety about professional presentations is that people are often concerned that they will appear as if they do not know what they are talking about; they're worried that they will look unprepared and unprofessional. The biggest fear is that an audience member will ask the dreaded question along the lines of, "Didn't Finkelstein and Berkowitz show just the opposite 10 years ago?" So, to overcome this, people work hard in their preparation, gather all of the relevant information that they can so that no one dare ask the question. Gathering the information is essential; you must know your topic area inside and out before you speak to a professional audience. However, telling your audience all of this information is both nonessential and, frankly, boring. No one wants to know your encyclopedia skills. A professional audience is willing to believe you too are professional, and it is often necessary for you to present only a few key papers or facts from your relevant topic area. Of course, you still may get the dreaded question, but because you *did* do your thorough literature search prior to your presentation, you can deal with it. But there is no need for you to go through every single previously known fact about your topic area so as to preempt this question. You'll confuse and bore your audience, and you'll run out of time to talk about your own work.

There is another question that is dreaded by professionals who present research data. This one comes in the form of, "Did you test your data for homoscedasticity?" How many of us have only a cursory knowledge of statistics and don't want to get caught out as novices? So, in hopes of fending off the question, we dazzle the audience with numbers—so many that they don't have time to determine whether we've conducted our analyses appropriately or not. But again, like demonstrating encyclopedia skills, this will only confuse and bore the audience. Of course, under all circumstances, it is *essential* that you understand fully your data analyses, the assumptions of these analyses, why you did one set of analyses and not another, and so on. If you have trouble with these things, get help before conducting your analyses in the first place. However, it is not essential to tell the audience all of this information. Again, professional audiences are willing to believe you have behaved in a professional manner, including conducting the appropriate analyses. The dreaded statistics question may still come, but the preemptive strike is unnecessary; the people who ask these questions will ask them no matter what. So be prepared. Have all of the statistical analyses written out in your notes; have additional overheads packed full of numbers to be shown only in response to the dreaded question; have a thorough understanding of what you did. But, in the first instance, present only the information that is needed to make your primary point (unless your primary point *is* about statistics, of course!).

The right goals

So what are the *right* goals in giving a professional presentation? The first and foremost goal is to communicate to your audience *your contribution as a professional*. What did you discover in your research? What new clinical findings have you uncovered? What insights have you developed, and what are the new directions they will take both you and the profession? It is the answers to these and similar questions that you should be presenting to your audience. Surprising as it may be to you, the audience has come to see and hear *you*; they believe you have something to tell them that they do not yet know, and they are willing to listen and learn. So give them what they've come for: your discoveries and insights, not your encyclopedia or statistical skills, just the hard facts that you are there to convey. This is what it is all about. Don't be shy—both you and your audience are there for a reason. If you have been invited to give your presentation, then someone obviously wants to hear you. If you are presenting at a professional seminar or conference, the mere presence of the audience confirms their interest.

Of course, I would be foolish and misleading to tell you that audiences are simply passive recipients of your information. They will attend to and think about what you say, and evaluate it (see "Thinking and nonthinking audiences" in chapter 4). And, like it or not, they will attend to *how* you say it, and evaluate that too. So, the second goal you should have when giving professional presentations is that of communicating the impression of yourself and your work that you want your audience to have; this second goal is that of *correct impression management*. Like it or not, enough intuition and social-psychological research tells us that we will be evaluated by our audiences. I learned this lesson early in my career, when, the day after I made my presentation at a professional conference, a stranger came up to me to tell me how much he enjoyed my presentation. This complete stranger thought I was great, despite his admission that he did not understand what I said! Now, this second part was a bit frustrating (and I hope that what I say in this book will help overcome audience confusion), but it made this man's admiration for me even more astounding. I realized then that you may be the most brilliant person, but if you come across to your audience as boring, aloof, nervous, or incompetent, not only will they not pay attention to you now, but they won't pay attention to you in the future. And if you come across well, your audience will want more. This is all the more important if your audience is comprised of people who can control your future (e.g., hiring you, promoting you, giving you money).

As shallow as it may appear, you have to come across to your audience in a professional and interesting manner. It may be nice in principle to say that people should like us just the way we are and that they should find what we have to say intrinsically interesting, but in reality, only our mothers think this. For everyone else, we have to work at giving clear and interesting presentations. In this book, I will outline some of the basic lessons.

SUMMARY TABLE 1.1 Know your goals of your presentation

Wrong goals

- Demonstrating encyclopedia skills
- Demonstrating statisitical and methodological skills

Right goals

- Communicating your contributions as a professional
- Communicating the impression you want to your audience

Writing your presentation

Writing a professional presentation involves more craft than people often think. In fact, by not recognizing this, people often encounter at least two common pitfalls. The first is when people recognize their own expertise and then assume they can speak extemporaneously, or "wing it." The second is when people write their presentations in the same structure and detail as they do for their professional articles and other written papers. These are both important "nos."

Writing pitfall 1: Extemporaneous presentations

Speaking extemporaneously is one of the worst things you can do. You will skip important information, backtrack to fill in information you missed earlier, stutter and stumble, lead the audience off onto tangents as you remember one thing or another, go over your time limit or end embarrassingly early, and generally fail to get even your most simple points across in a clear manner. This is the same even for those great orators who appear to be speaking off the top of their heads. Don't be fooled; what they're saying has previously been written and rehearsed, and you need to do the same too. Again, I learned this lesson early in my career when, during my first presentation at my first job I thought I could "wing it." It was a disaster, as I made almost every error I listed above, plus some! It is essential that you prepare what you are going to say in detail before you say it. If you can memorize your whole talk so that you appear to be speaking extemporaneously, then more power to you. In whatever manner you do it, however, your presentation must be extemporaneous in appearance only.

Writing pitfall 2: Presentations as written papers

As students, we often learn to write papers in a specific style that allows for the clearest exposition of ideas. If it is research that we're writing about, then we know to start with an introduction, move to the methods, then to results, and end with a discussion.[1] Following these guidelines when writing papers is fine, and even good. The basic outline is logical, clear, and generally expected from your audience. However, there is a lot of information that is typically included in written papers that should be kept out of professional presentations. In written text, it is easy for your audience to contemplate all of this information, because they can move through your ideas at their own pace, and go back to previous pages if necessary to understand fully what you are saying. But when presenting this information in verbal form, it is very difficult to attend to everything and follow what you are saying. So some things need to be cut.

Telling you exactly what to cut, as a general rule, is very difficult because it will always depend on the content of your topic and the nature of your audience. In principle, however, you should keep out the excruciating details. These can include (surprisingly) a thorough literature review, the number of participants and why they participated, the exact number of questions on your questionnaire, every previous study that used your questionnaire, all conceivable statistics about your questionnaire and its results, and all possible flaws in your study. You should not misunderstand what I'm saying. Each one of these things is very important, and in your written report you must include them all. Moreover, there are times when you should say them in your professional presentation too, such as when your topic and results are particularly controversial, your methods novel, and your participants sampled from a special population. However, in most circumstances, these kinds of details often detract from the *content* of your presentation. Remember that your goal is to present your contribution to your profession, and not to present your encyclopedia or statistical skills. Not only should you not substitute form for substance, you should not detract from substance with form. And "wowing them with statistics," for example, as a ploy to fend off the hard questions about content, is destined only to backfire when the statistics expert in the audience raises her hand to query what you've done!

What you should do: Tell a story

Unlike extemporaneous or written-paper-like presentations, probably one of the most important things you can do when giving a professional presentation is tell a story. You can not assume that your audience will automatically be interested in the specific topic you will be talking about (see "Your similarity to your audience" in chapter 4). Although this comes as a surprise to some people, it's definitely true. So, like a good storyteller, you have to attract the attention of your audience and engage them in the unfolding of your ideas. This may sound like I'm considering audiences to be fickle, but maintaining the attention of your audience is an art in itself (especially if your presentation is over 30 minutes long). And reviewing a long list of facts, no matter how important you think they are, will fail to interest your audience.

First of all, when giving your presentation, you have to tell your audience why they should be interested in what you have to say. It's not enough to assume that the audience will find interesting and exciting the same things you do; a simple reflection on watching other people's holiday slide shows is enough to confirm this! Broad categories like "helping people" or "theoretically interesting" or "empirically interesting" are not enough. The manner in which help is provided to people—and, indeed, what constitutes help—is always value bound, and your audience may not share your values. And, of course, what is and is not "interesting" remains, too, a matter of the audience's values and general preferences. All this means that you should *know a bit about your audience* before giving your presentation, and this means a bit of homework. If you can introduce your work with reference to the kinds of things your audience is likely to value (even if you did not consider these thing in the first place), then you will find that you have a much more attentive and interested audience. Of course, it is not always possible to tie your work into the direct interests of your audience (if only because it will seem forced and, hence, insincere). In such instances, you may want to begin your presentation with an anecdote of some kind as if you are just chatting with the audience. Anecdotes can include recent news items, your own personal experiences, and even some observations you have made about your profession. Note, however, that it is essential that the anecdote *transparently* correspond to what you will ultimately say in the rest of your presentation. Opening with jokes in attempts to get laughs will only make you look foolish and annoy your audience if the jokes have no connection to any other feature of what you will say (see "Humor" in chapter 4). But well-told anecdotes can actually *foreshadow* many of the topics you will consider in your presentation.

Consider the following two ways of starting off presentations about the same topic in social psychology. The first is actual text I have used to describe my own research in written form; remember, in written form, text can be relatively complex. The second is the way I have started professional presentations in the past of the exact same material as described in the first text.

In my ongoing research, I have examined people's responses to others' use and non-use of prescriptive fairness rules across different social situations. Prescriptive fairness rules, in this research, derived from formal interpersonal distributive justice theories. One rule, for example, is equality (each person receives equal amounts), and another is equity (each person receives proportionally to his or her contribution). When varying the use of these rules across different social situations, an apparent paradox appeared. In one instance, people responded favorably to prescriptive fairness in intragroup situations; these situations are ones in which the people involved in the resource distribution are all members of the same group (e.g., same university, same country, same laboratory work group). In another instance, however, people responded favorably to prescriptive unfairness in intergroup situations; these situations are ones in which the people involved in the resource distribution are members of different groups.

Okay, if you didn't yawn or get lost through that, I'll be surprised. But now consider the following introduction to an oral presentation of the same material.

Several years ago, when I was a graduate student, a few men decided that the best way they could demonstrate their loyalty and patriotism to the United States was to violate congressional law, usurp the constitution, establish their own separate powers, sell arms to Iran, and channel the proceeds to the former Somozitas—or "Contras"—in Nicaragua. You may remember this as the "Iran-Contra Scandal." One of the key players in this was Oliver North, who testified in front of Congress and the whole of the American public, saying he did what he did because of "them," because of the communists. So, here we had an American, an "in-group member"—clearly identified by the highly decorated military uniform he wore—who displayed "in-group favoritism" by saying, essentially, "We're better than them," who was liked by the public, who the public wanted to be president, and who was actually persuasive in what he said. Now the research that I will present today tries to provide some answers to why this "Oliver North Effect" may occur—why people like, want to vote for, and are persuaded by in-group members who display strong in-group favoritism, even if, in other circumstances, they think this behavior is unfair.

This introduction was highly successful over several occasions. It didn't matter if the audience was comprised of social psychologists or not, or of Americans or not, the anecdote succeeded in capturing people's attention and led them to want to know more. Once the anecdote was presented, however, I moved straight into the professional information. I would ultimately discuss all the information presented in the first introduction above, but when I did so, I made reference not only to published theory and research, but to my anecdote; so now, rather than being complex, my presentation came across as almost intuitive.

Once you have grabbed your audience's attention and interest, you still have to maintain it. One way of doing this is to remember the "don'ts" and "pitfalls" listed above; don't bore your audience with a long review of the history of your topic, or of complex statistics, or of details that are not essential to get across your primary message. In addition, however, don't tell your "punch line" at the beginning so you have nothing left to say. I was at a presentation once where the speaker announced his main findings in the first five minutes of a 50-minute talk. After that, the rest of the talk was uneventful, as the author worked his way through all the pitfalls of the study. By the end, I (and the rest of the audience) was no longer impressed! So the lesson is *build up* to your main point. Raise meaningful questions and problems that face your discipline, and consider the potential solutions that others have offered (see "Asking rhetorical quesitons" in chapter 4). Ultimately, these potential solutions will be straw men, but certainly not disingenuous ones. You should be considering honest explanations to your quandary, but typically there is only one reason you are in front of the audience to begin with—because you have a new answer to offer. So as you show the inadequacy of each alternative (of each antagonist in your story) you lead the audience to one final solution, the one you provided (your protagonist). If you follow this procedure, I recommend introducing your new solution about one-third of your way through your talk—any earlier, and you'll end your talk too soon; any later and your audience will wonder if you have anything new to say.

Of course, it will almost always be the case that you will not have the final answer to the problems posed in your discipline. That's fine. But you should structure your presentation in such a way your new work *does* answer the questions you posed initially to your audience. The worst situation is to leave your audience with unanswered questions that you posed to them; if you can't answer the question, don't pose it. This, of course, does not mean that at the very end (in your denouement) you cannot pose new questions for future directions. You can, but pose them at the end; the audience will understand that you haven't an immediate answer to them.

In sum, like any good story, you want a way of bringing your audience into your grips within the first few minutes of speaking. This can easily be done with a simple anecdote that will illustrate the points you will eventually make. You then want to set the stage with the antagonists in the form of alternative theories and ideas beating hard at the problem, but failing. Your new ideas, your protagonist, should be introduced to answer the question, to "save the townsfolk." And the new questions posed at the end hint at future adventures for your protagonist. But be mindful: I am not instructing you to tell stories for the sake of storytelling. Your professional audience is not comprised of children. Remember the goals of communicating your contribution as a professional and communicating the impression you want to your audience. Storytelling is a method of exposition, one that will provide you with structure and form while allowing you to maintain the attention and interest of your audience.

What you should do: Assume sophistication in your audience

The advice to assume sophistication in your audience may sound a bit at odds with the previous advice to tell a story. What I mean, however, is that you can assume a specific level of shared knowledge in your audience. Of course, this means knowing something about your audience in the first place. So if your audience is comprised of professional researchers, then you probably do not have to describe the details of your statistical analyses; the audience probably already knows. Basically, in any profession, there is a set of jargon that you can reasonably assume everyone knows. This is not just types of statistics, but methods, theories, and so on. I observed once a speaker who went into excruciating detail on a 20-year-old research method, one that most people in the audience had actually used in the past. She bored the audience and wasted her own time, leaving less time for her new contributions. Basically, explaining known information and jargon conveys a message to your audience that you think *they* are not professionals, bores your audience, and wastes precious time in your own presentation. So, it is okay to assume some sophistication in your audience. If you do say something that they do not know, they'll ask; in response, simply apologize and explain.

Of course, there are times when you will be speaking to nonprofessional, lay audiences or audiences in professions other than your own. In these cases, it may be necessary to do a bit more explaining. But again, know your audience, and why they're listening to you. If you are presenting your ideas to the Elks Club, then you still do not have to explain the details of your statistical analyses; they don't want to know.

What you should do: Present a subset of your work only

It is very unlikely that the work you are engaged in is limited in method and scope. And it is equally unlikely that you can actually do complete justice to your work in the typical 50-minute presentation, let alone 15- or 20-minute presentations. So, you *must* present only a subset of your work. You just don't have time to present all relevant details. Don't think you can get around the issue simply by speaking faster. I saw a speaker once announce that her presentation took 50 minutes, despite being given only 20 minutes to talk. Her solution: Talk fast. Needless to say, the speed with which she spoke and displayed her overhead slides was beyond my comprehension, and I'm sure most of the audience's too. This author clearly couldn't "bare the knife" in cutting down her presentation, and left only confusion in her wake. Cutting, however, is essential.

When writing your professional presentation, you must select either specific highlights across your entire topic area or one or two points out of many. This doesn't mean that the topics you are leaving out are unimportant; you probably could just as easily write a presentation with these points alone too. One reason we often find cutting quite difficult is because we know that one or another topic that we may leave out of the presentation may leave us open to greater criticism from our audience. Because we have left out some of the information, the audience will necessarily be getting only a partial glimpse at our work and will undoubtedly be wondering why we didn't do a complete job. But to our rescue is our knowledge that we *did* do a complete job; we've just decided to present only a subset. So when the question comes from the audience that, "Well, that's all interesting and nice, but I'm not persuaded because you haven't dealt with the 'ramphramizam' issue," we need only reply, "Excellent point. In fact, I *did* deal with that issue and can speak to it during the question period at the end of my presentation. I've just left it out of the main presentation in the interests of presenting a simple line of thought." It's as simple as that.

So, the lesson is, identify the one or two main points you want to make in your presentation, and make them. The rest of your work will wait for your next presentation, or for that critical question that may or may not come. This means cutting and streamlining to make a story with a single and simple plot.

What you should do: Write to your time limit

Closely aligned with the ideas of presenting a subset of your work is writing to your time limit. It is important enough, however, for me to state it explicitly. Anytime you are asked to give a professional presentation, you will be told how long you will be expected to speak. If you are not told, ask. Unlike our infamous speaker above, you do not want to arrive prepared to give a 50-minute presentation only to find out you have only 20 minutes to speak. At the same time, you do not want the opposite to happen. Speaking for only 20 minutes when your audience is expecting 50 minutes is not any better. Your presentation and your ideas will end with a fizzle rather than a bang as your audience waits for you to tell more, not realizing you have finished. I have seen this too, and it is very awkward for all involved, as the audience members, presentation convenor, or both desperately try to think of questions to ask the speaker to use up more of the allotted time. Don't think speaking for less time will get you out of the hot seat faster; it won't. So, again, write to your time limit. But how will you know how long your presentation will take? The answer is very simple: Practice before you give it.

What you should do: Practice

If you were hoping that you would find advice on "positive imagery" and "mental rehearsals" in this book, your hopes will be dashed. My advice is more old-fashioned and, frankly, more worthwhile. It is, too, more effort. The advice is simple: Practice. Practice your talk, and not just in your head. Practice your talk out loud, and do it several times. The adage is right: Practice makes perfect. This is the only way that your presentation will run smoothly in front of your actual audience. Elite athletes may, indeed, use positive imagery to fine-tune their performances, but the bulk of their success—certainly over 95% of it—comes from their repeated actual practice. And practice is where the bulk of your success will come from too.

Practice is important for several reasons. First, although we speak every day, we often don't listen to ourselves. When practicing out loud to an empty room, we can do nothing but listen to ourselves. And if you're like me, you'll shudder when you hear yourself! You'll stutter, you'll stumble, and you'll "um" and "ahh." You won't be able to tell the story you want, and you'll feel like a fool. *But it's no problem. You'll be alone; no one will hear you.* This is the time to make your mistakes. And this is the time to correct them. So, by practicing out loud, you are, effectively, rehearsing your performance. You will be able to get your words out correctly, to say them with the vocal intonations you want and in the order that you want.

This last point, saying your words in the order you want, is the second important reason for practicing. Without practice, you may go into your actual presentation and forget to say one thing or another, so you stumble, recall, and backtrack to get it right. You don't want to do this. You want to say things correctly from the beginning. Practice will help you do this. (So will an organized talk and visual aids, described in the section of this chapter titled "Making overhead slides.") Only through actual practice will you learn your presentation. This may seem odd; there should be no reason to learn your presentation because you wrote it in the first place. However, when you stand up in front of an audience without practice, you will quickly realize that writing your presentation is no guarantee of knowing it. You will find, rather, that you have a broad knowledge of it, but the finer details will elude you when the pressure is on. The primary way around this is by practice. By practice, you will begin to memorize your presentation. Now, I'm not asking you to engage in rote memorization, but memorization is what you will achieve with practice. You'll know what to say next; you'll know what is on your overheads; you'll know what the facts, ideas, and numbers are. You won't hesitate, you won't stumble, and you won't stutter. And, you will feel and be more confident.

The third reason to practice your presentation is not just to help you come to grips with your content, but also with the physical equipment that you will use during your presentation. Professional presentations can certainly be lost (although not necessarily made) on how the presenter interacts with his or her equipment. Fumbling around with slide projectors, PowerPoint equipment, and even simple overheads wastes time and makes you look foolish. And don't be misled; bumbling around with the equipment will *not* make you appear like the endearing, bumbling genius. So when you practice your presentation, do so with the equipment you will use (or the best possible at your disposal). I will give you advice later in this chapter and in the next on making and using visual aids. But the point here is simply that the equipment will be an integral part of your presentation, and you must practice using it when practicing the presentation.

The fourth reason to practice your presentation is to help you organize your time. I made a strong point above about writing your presentation to your time limit. But you will have no idea how much time you will take unless you actually take the time during your practice. So do it, and if it's too long, then cut; if it's too short, add.

So, the advice is this: Practice your full presentation multiple times, out loud, with an overhead, slide, or PowerPoint projector.

What you should do: Lecture from overheads, slides, or PowerPoint displays

Lecturing from overheads, slides, or PowerPoint displays is extremely valuable, especially for people without a lot of practice with professional presentations. These visual aids not only will help your audience follow along, but will help you too. These will serve as your notes. Of course, one way to write a professional presentation is to write word for word what you will say, and then read it to your audience. This is certainly a good idea *as a back-up plan* in case you freeze with stage fright (see "Do not read word for word" and "Stage fright" in chapter 2), but reading your presentation will only bore your audience. You will have a tendency to read too fast, to speak in a monotone, and never to look at your audience. You will, in essence, be placing the burden on the audience to follow what you are saying. The burden, however, should be on you to lead the audience. So use visual aids as short notes to both the audience and yourself. These short notes will be cues to you for what you should say. In the next section, I will describe in detail how you should make your visual aids.

SUMMARY TABLE 1.2 Writing your presentation

What you should not do (Pitfalls)

- Give your presentations extemporaneously
- Give your presentations as written papers

What you should do

- Tell a story
- Assume sophistication in your audience
- Present a subset of your work only
- Write to your time limit
- Practice
- Lecture from overheads, slides, or PowerPoint displays

Making overheads and slides

Keep your information at a minimum

As I said earlier, your overheads, slides, and PowerPoint displays should be short notes to your audience and yourself. This means that you should not overwhelm your audience with information. Do not include your word-for-word text—possibly a single sentence here and there, but that's all. With too much information on the projection screen, your audience will be reading rather than listening to you. The suggestions I make below focus particularly on the use of overheads. I do this because after much use of other media (including PowerPoint), I am convinced that overheads remain the best medium for presentations, if only for clarity and ease of use. Indeed, overhead projectors are far easier to use and seem to be in working order more often than either slide projectors or PowerPoint facilities. Having said this, all of the information I present in this section is directly relevant to slide usage and PowerPoint displays. I also have a separate section in this chapter on PowerPoint, but it should not be read without also reading this current section.

Write in short points

When preparing your overheads, slides, and PowerPoint displays, write in short points. Decide what the main ideas are that you want your audience to know at each stage of your story, and distill those ideas into a few short words. Of course, this is easier said than done, but it is your responsibility to do the work, not your audience's. If you don't do the distilling, you will be putting the burden of cognitive effort onto your audience, and they'll quickly fatigue. The distilling is often most difficult in your areas of expertise because you know all of the nuances and that "life is not so simple." However, if you start telling your audience all of the nuances, your ultimate conclusion will be arrived at only through a weaving and winding path, leaving the audience more dizzy than informed. Of course, if there are important qualifications to your points, then definitely make them; I am not telling you to mislead your audience. But it is okay to have a ceteris paribus—all else being equal—assumption in your work. If not, you will never get around to making your point. Remember, the overheads are guides for your audience. You can think of them as a type of map. We know that road maps are highly distilled representations of all of the nuances of reality. They don't tell us about the buildings, the road construction, the felled road signs, the traffic conditions, and so on; but they do aid us in getting to our destination. It is the same with your overheads—they should aid your audience (and you) in getting to the final destination of your presentation.

Tables of numbers should be simple or absent

Tables of numbers are often very enticing because of our desire to present all relevant information. But more often than not, there is just too much information. And with so many numbers, the audience does not know where to look. Of course, to you, they are all so clear, but that's because you've had hours, days, and months to consider them; the audience only has minutes. If you need to display quantitative information, it will be easiest for your audience if you present it in the form of a figure (i.e., a graph). The pictorial representation will typically be a simplification of your information. You will, thus, be leaving out the finer details, but you will gain by making salient the essence of what you want your audience to know. Again, if it is essential that the audience knows the minute details, then present them; but think long and hard about it beforehand. If you present too many numbers, then your audience will comprehend neither the essence of what you want nor the finer details. If you want, you can make one or two reserve overheads or slides with all of the tables of numbers that you want. You would use these reserves *only* when asked for greater detail by your audience. If the audience doesn't ask for them, don't show them; but you'll have the tables ready if the audience does ask. Later in this chapter, I provide some suggestions on making graphs.

Do not include inferential statistics

We often rely on inferential statistics as types of persuasion cues, almost as if saying to our audience, "If it's statistically significant, then it must be true." So what typically happens is that the less confident we are in our own professional ideas, the more statistics we throw at the audience. This approach, however, can easily backfire (see "The wrong goals" earlier in this chapter). It is the same point I am making throughout this section. Too much information will not persuade your audience; it will only confuse them. And, in the end, in a professional presentation it is not *necessary* for you to use these persuasion cues to increase your credibility (see "Your similarity to your audience" in chapter 4). If you say, "Group A was more/bigger/greater than Group B," then you have stated what you believe to be true. Your professional audience will believe you are behaving professionally and not lying. If you have drawn a graph of your data, this should make it all the clearer. Indeed, one editor of a psychology journal explicitly asked for graphs rather than inferential statistics as an editorial policy.[2] Of course, like your tables of numbers, you can have reserve overheads with all of the inferential statistics written on them when the audience asks for them. But, in the meantime, keep them off your principal overheads and slides; they only add to the clutter.

Do not include names and dates

Like inferential statistics, we often rely on names and dates as types of persuasion cues. We are often afraid to speak our own minds during professional presentations in case someone criticizes us as being wrong. So, instead, we say, "Smith said this in 1968, and Jones said it again in 1975, but more recently, it was said by Silverstein and Goldsmith in 1999." The implication, of course, is that if all these famous and intelligent people said so, then it must be true; so don't blame me! If you want to show the historical progression of thought or give credit to those who deserve it, then fine. But keep off of your overheads as many names and dates as possible; they'll just clutter them up. Anyway, your audience is present to see you and to hear *your* views. Remember, demonstrating your encyclopedia skills is not one of your goals.

Do not include other needless details

This final point is more of a catchall for anything that I have left out, and a reminder to keep your overheads simple. If it is not *critical* to your main point that "213 participants between the ages of 17 and 54 participated as part of a class requirement," then keep this information—and other information like it—off your overheads. Another common bit of needless information is cartoons. Sometimes cartoons can, indeed, be helpful in telling your story. However, if the cartoons are not directly relevant, if you will not address the cartoon issues directly in your presentation, then drop them. Having cartoons for entertainment purposes only detracts from what you are going to say. The same goes for opening quotes from famous people. Often, presenters begin their presentation with a quote that they think is rather insightful. But, again, if it is not directly relevant, don't say it, and definitely do not put it on your overheads.

Keep your overheads, slides, and PowerPoint displays in a structured format

When using overheads, slides, and PowerPoint displays, your audience will be spending a great deal of time attending to and reading them. If the format on your visual aids is unstructured, so too will be your overall presentation. Although *you* might know the structure—where you're going to and where you've come from—your audience will not know. To the audience, the visual aids *are* the presentation. Unstructured overheads, slides, and PowerPoint displays make unstructured presentations.

Have a meaningful title

This advice may sound self-evident, but far too often, people opt for the "cute and catchy" title instead of the informative title. A meaningful title, however, is essential. It will tell your audience exactly what you will be talking about. It will give them some insight into the direction of your story. In contrast, cute titles run the risk of being cute only to you, while certainly being uninformative. So stay with the meaningful title.

State your objective, the general context, or framework

The first content you should have on your visual aids (after your title, name, and affiliation) is the basic objective of your presentation, or the general context or framework within which you will be speaking. This need not (and, indeed, should not) be lengthy. But, like the importance of a meaningful title, you want to tell your audience immediately what you will be discussing. Undoubtedly, you will need to go into greater detail during the remainder of your presentation (or else you would have no presentation!), but simply foreshadowing your objectives or the context of your work will aid your audience in following your presentation. Not stating your objectives until midway through the presentation or assuming that your audience will infer the general context is simply asking your audience to do too much work. Just tell them; and do so in the beginning and in simple terms (see "Stating your position ahead of time and drawing conclusions at the end" in chapter 4).

Separate your presentation into meaningful sections

Separating your presentation into meaningful sections achieves some of the cognitive work for your audience. Having a continuous list of ideas and facts on your overheads requires your audience to infer the meaningful similarities and differences between your points. *You* should be stating these similarities and differences, and you can do it easily by creating different sections of your presentation. For a research presentation, of course, there are the basic "Introduction," "Methods," "Results," and "Discussion." However, you can go farther by breaking down the different components of each of these—and similar—sections, highlighting differences of fact, perspective, and argument. These different sections should be written on your overheads, each, of course, with meaningful titles. The easiest way to make these different sections clear to your audience is by using an outline form.

Use an outline form

Using an outline form when writing your overheads, slides and PowerPoint displays will provide the clearest presentation of your ideas to your audience. Because of its ordered nature, using an outline form will also assist you to write the most structured presentation you can. The outline form thus assists both you and your audience. I have used an outline form in writing the chapters of this book. Notice that each chapter is broken down into sections and subsections. The goal is to provide some sort of guide to the reader. In fact, if I were to write the chapters as a professional presentation, then each of the headings and subheadings would be written on my overheads, and the text describing them would be the actual content of what I say.

Forget the fancy stuff

With the advent of such things as color printers, clip art, and PowerPoint, people may feel compelled to move from the more simple overheads of the past to some real fancy stuff to "wow" the audience. Don't be fooled. The fancy stuff rarely impresses a professional audience. More often than not, it actually detracts from the content of what you have to say. My advice is to keep your visual aids as simple as possible. Of course, there are times when, say, the addition of color to graphs will aid in reading; by all means, go ahead and use it. But adding color, animation (on PowerPoint), and the like just for the sake of it will win you no points with your audience.

I should point out, however, one caveat to my general prohibition on fancy stuff. You *may* actually find yourself preparing a professional presentation for an audience that actually expects the fancy stuff. I shudder at this thought and think it's quite a shame, but I do realize it is true. So, as I have said previously, know your audience. Sometimes people do want more glitter than gold, so give them the glitter. But honestly, I'd venture a guess that in 90% of your professional presentations, your audience will want the gold and could not care less about the glitter. Your audience will be interested in your contributions to your profession, and not, for example, your expertise at PowerPoint.

Write your overheads, slides, and PowerPoint displays in sequential format

My advice to write your overheads, slides, and PowerPoint displays in sequential format may sound redundant with that of using outline form. However, I am talking about something different here. When you begin your presentation, you will have a pile of overheads, a slide tray full of slides, or your PowerPoint presentation all ready to go. My advice here is to work your way through each overhead or slide and *not to go back*. Sometimes presenters will have one major figure that will exemplify ideas throughout the presentation. These presenters will make one overhead or slide of this figure and then return to it again and again as they speak. The problem here is either that the overhead gets lost in the pile of already-used overheads, or they'll have to work their way through a tray full of slides to get back to the figure, and so on. The fact is, going back to a previously used overhead or slide is clumsy and cumbersome, and it wastes time. If you need to refer to a particular piece of information more than once, then simply repeat this information on new overheads or slides. It may sound like a waste of resources, but it is not; waste will come only if it has no use in your presentation.

So when writing your overheads, slides, or PowerPoint displays, make each one to be used in sequence. When you are done with each overhead, you can place it in a pile that will not be used again until the question period at the end. During your presentation, all you will have to remember is to keep progressing through your unused overheads or slides. Because you will have organized them all prior to your presentation, you know that you will never have to fiddle around looking for that "one important figure." I have seen too many talks fall apart because the speaker loses the all-important overhead and spends five minutes searching, offering embarrassed explanations. If the speaker had only written each overhead in sequence, rather than planning on moving back and forth, the presentation would have been perfect.

Font type and size

Another one of the big mistakes presenters often make is to take their 12-point, Times Roman–typed manuscripts and photocopy the text onto overheads for their presentations. Unless the audience is sitting where the presenter is standing, then the text is impossible to read. Doing this is, frankly, discourteous to the audience by making them strain unnecessarily. In this section, I have some practical advice for font types and sizes.

Font type

When preparing your overheads, you should use a **sans serif** font. This is the type of font that does *not* have the small tails and curli-cues on each letter. Examples of sans serif fonts are **Helvetica** and **Arial**. Although most books (like this one) and professional papers are written in serif fonts such as Times Roman, these are not necessarily the best for overheads and slides. Research has actually shown that, at least with low luminance, **sans serif** fonts are easier to read.[3] Given that you often won't know the quality of the equipment you will be using when you give your professional presentation, it's best to use the **sans serif** fonts only.

Font size

Of course, there is not one standard rule I can tell you in terms of font size that will be appropriate for all presentations, formats, projection screens, and lecture theaters. The most I can do is provide you with some suggestions based on my previous successes. The main point to remember is that typical manuscript fonts of 10-point and 12-point are *definitely* too small for overheads, slides, and PowerPoint displays; with these small fonts, your audience will not read what you have written. So my recommendations are to use 36- to 48-point bold fonts for your main headings, 28-point bold fonts for your first sublevel headings, 28-point plain (nonbold) fonts for your second sub-level headings, and 22- to 24-point plain fonts for your third sublevel headings. These font sizes should be quite satisfactory for your audience to read your overheads.

Readability: Spacing, emphasis, and printing

When writing your overheads, slides, and PowerPoint displays, remember that the goal is for your audience to be able to read what you have written. One big mistake people often make is to clutter their overheads and slides by placing too much information on them. You should avoid this in at least two ways. First, always use *at least* double-spacing; single-spacing will make it simply too hard to read. Second, if you want to emphasize a point, **bold** rather than <u>underline</u> or *italicize*. Underlining simply places more marks on your overheads and slides, and italics may sometimes be difficult to read.

One last point I want to make is simple, but needs to be said. When making overhead projections, make sure you use a high-quality printer. Old-fashioned dot-matrix printers, or printers running out of ink or in need of servicing should definitely not be used. Poor-quality printouts make poor-quality overheads.

SUMMARY TABLE 1.3 Making overheads and slides

Keep your information at a minimum

- Write in short points
- Have a meaningful title
- State your objective, the general context, or framework
- Separate your presentation into meaningful sections
- Use an outline form
- Forget the fancy stuff
- Write your overheads in sequential format

Choose an appropriate font type and size

- Use sans serif fonts (e.g., Arial or Helvetica)
- Use large font sizes
- Write clear and uncluttered overheads and slides

Working with PowerPoint

My advice earlier was to "forget the fancy stuff." PowerPoint, however, is part of that "fancy stuff." So why this section? The answer, simply, is that a lot of people want to use PowerPoint but would like or could benefit from some tips. You'll notice, however, that my advice is rather brief; I have limited what I've said to a few tips that should help you get started. A detailed account of how to use PowerPoint is really the topic of a completely separate book. My goal currently is to provide you with some basics on giving good professional presentations. So, of course, you must read this section in conjunction with the entireties of chapters 1, 2, and 3 for your best chance at a successful presentation.

I should say, at this point, that my discussion of PowerPoint is not an endorsement of one specific piece of software over others. PowerPoint is a Microsoft product. There may be other presentation software available that is just as good if not better; my advice here should cover that other software too. Again, my focus on PowerPoint is the simple recognition that a lot of people currently want to use it.

Why you might want to use PowerPoint

After having used PowerPoint on several occasions for at least the past three years, I've come to believe that there are a few aspects of the real-time computer presentation that can, in fact, facilitate professional presentations.

Hyperlinks

Earlier in this chapter, I said that you should write your overheads, slides, and PowerPoint displays in a sequential format. Following this advice will allow you not to get lost and not to waste time going back and forth between current displays and previous ones. Hyperlinks, however, are features that can make moving around in a nonsequential format a lot easier. Hyperlinks are simply instructions to the computer to move either to a specific slide within your display, a specific computer file, or a specific Internet address. By establishing your hyperlinks when you are first writing your presentation, you can overcome the foibles of getting lost between slides and yet be freed from a nonsequential format (if you are moving within your display). This, of course, takes a lot of a priori preparation time, and you remain bound to what you have instructed the computer to do. In the end, my advice remains *not* to hyperlink within your own presentation; if you want to use the same PowerPoint slide more than once, simply copy it into the appropriate place in your sequential format.

Hyperlinks come into their own, however, when you want to move *out* of your presentation. If you want to move into a specific Web site, for example, using PowerPoint as your mode of presentation means you already have a computer turned on and projected to your audience. With a simple mouse click, your audience can be viewing the Internet site within seconds. Don't forget, of course, that if your host's computer is not connected to the Internet, then your Internet hyperlink will be completely useless. The same can be said for when the server at your host institution or the Web site itself is down at the time of your presentation. These problems are things well beyond your control, so use your hyperlinks to the outside world sparingly and only to facilitate the point you are trying to make. If you can make your point without the hyperlink, all the better. Remember, your audience is not interested in how well you can surf around the net. But if you want to get to an Internet site—for example, an Internet experiment, a data bank, references, continually updated statistics—then having your presentation computer-based from the beginning will be a great time saver and will allow you not to fumble between different pieces of equipment.

Multimedia

Another time that PowerPoint comes into its own is with the use of multimedia presentations. With advances in computer technology, you can now relatively easily digitize sound and video clips and burn your digital files onto compact disks. I've done this myself for some of my classroom presentations (see chapter 5). With PowerPoint, you can present your normal text information, but you can also establish a link to your sound and video clips. So, again, with this feature, you can start your video clips, for example, with a simple mouse click, instead of having to switch between different pieces of equipment. Of course, you'll need to ensure that your display computer is connected to an adequate speaker system; check this with your host *before* you arrive for your presentation.

Working with PowerPoint features

Simply by opening up PowerPoint for the first time, you'll notice a wide variety of features. In this section, I discuss seven very simple ones that will be handy to get you started and help you avoid problems I've seen in the past.

Introducing text systematically

In chapter 2, I will advise you to reveal your visual information to your audience slowly. PowerPoint has a feature ("Introduce Text") that will allow you to specify whether you want the entire slide presented all at once, or specific features one at a time. You should use the one-at-a-time feature (found under "custom animation"), grouping text by the paragraph points you make. This will allow your audience to focus on the specific topic you're speaking on at that time.

Colors

As soon as you move away from traditional overheads, the wonderful world of color is open to you. Color can be a great facilitator for you. For example, when emphasizing a specific point, rather than bolding (as I recommend earlier in "Readability"), you can write the text in a different color; as with boldface type, this will make your emphasis salient without cluttering the screen with underlines or making the text harder to read with italics. Beware, however; there are at least two problems people often encounter when the full color palette is at their fingertips.

The first problem people often encounter when moving away from simple black text on a white background is that of *contrast*. More correctly, the problem is really one of lack of contrast. The text that will be easiest for your audience to read is that of the highest possible contrast (i.e., black and white). With colors now available to you, however, you may now want to have backgrounds other than "boring" white. In fact, Microsoft provides a variety of different templates for you to use in PowerPoint, each with different backgrounds in colors other than white. As soon as you move away from a white background with black text, however, you will be making your display harder for your audience to read (white text on a black background is, of course, also very high in contrast; however, many people may find this very awkward because most of us are used to reading black on white).

My suggestion is simple. If you want to add some colors, use a very pale blue, pink, or tan as your background. Then stick to black text, or highly saturated blues and reds. Never use red text on a blue background (or vice versa). I've seen this in the past, and it is just impossible to read. And remember, the colors you see on your computer screen in your office may not be the colors that are projected when you are in front of your audience (because of different computers and the quality of the projector). Finally, remember that several people have color deficiencies in their visual systems, resulting in a confusing of green, yellow, orange, and red; assuming equal luminance and color saturation, using one of these colors as text and another as background will render your display impossible to read for these people.

The second problem people encounter with the easy access of colors is their overuse. As I said above, the use of color is very handy if you want to emphasize a point. However, some presenters I have seen think that each new word or each new sentence is sufficiently important to have its own color. Unfortunately, the rainbow of colors presented on the screen (although possibly very pretty) is actually difficult to read, if only because the audience does not know which point is more important than the next. If the points are all equally important, then they should all be the same color. If you want to emphasize the points differentially, put them each on different slides. The rainbow, however, is only confusing.

Headings

When you write text within each PowerPoint slide, you do so within a specific text box. These boxes allow you to have specific text for specific reasons. For example, on most templates available on PowerPoint, there is a specific text box for a title or heading, and a specific text box for additional text or figures. The title/heading text boxes can come in handy if you continue a single point in your presentation over a series of PowerPoint slides. Say, for example, you wanted to discuss your research methods, but they were sufficiently complex that you needed five PowerPoint slides to make your point. In this case, you should use the title text box on each of the five slides, labeling it, in this case, "Methods." This serves as a reminder to your audience of your current topic. When you change topics (e.g., to "Results"), you should change the title too, again maintaining it for the whole section that it covers.

Animation

Like the availability of colors, the computer technology in PowerPoint allows you to add animation to your presentation. I have one simple piece of advice: Don't do it. I have seen too many PowerPoint presentations in which the speakers used all the different silly animation features available. I can assure you that it ends up as one muddled mess; it is difficult to attend to, and most audience members' opinions of the speaker drop as they begin to realize that the speaker spent more time playing with his or her computer than thinking, or (worse yet) that the speaker thinks of the audience more as children who need entertaining!

Having given you the general prohibition, if your urges to use the animation are too strong to resist, there are two forms of animation that I have found to be satisfactory *when presenting text*. The first is the "box out" animation. This is good for the initial presentation of titles; it begins writing the text from the middle, and expands out. The second type of animation is "wipe right." This is good for writing each of your outline points to the screen; it writes the text from left to right, much in the way that your audience will read it.

Chart effects

Chart effects are also forms of animation that I have found to be particularly useful in your presentation. When creating your chart (i.e., graph) in

PowerPoint, you do not have to have all data points presented to the screen as soon as the graph is displayed. Instead, you can write your display so that each data point is drawn to the screen with a separate mouse click. This is particularly nice because it allows you to speak about each separate condition or category of data prior to displaying it. This helps keep your audience's attention on what you are saying; when you have finished speaking, you can make your mouse click and display the next data point. This is a very good way of maintaining control during your presentation (see "Maintain control over your audience" in chapter 3).

Sounds

Microsoft has provided users with the ability to add specific sounds to their presentations, such as applause, a camera click, a drumroll, and breaking glass. I suppose the goal was to add a little flair to people's presentations. Unfortunately, in a professional context, use of these sounds will just make you look foolish. Don't use them. They detract from your presentation by the addition of unnecessary noise. They rarely, if ever, are related to the content of what you'll be speaking about. They are very common, so that most audience members will now be so familiar with them that they (the audience) will be bored rather than amused by them. Moreover, if you use drumrolls and applause on your own work, you'll just look conceited. I know that I outlined above that adding sounds to your presentations can be a positive multimedia feature of PowerPoint. However, in that case, I was speaking of sounds that were relevant to your work (e.g., an interview with an anonymous and consenting client).

Use the "pack and go" feature

This a very handy feature that the developers of PowerPoint have provided. When you have finished creating your PowerPoint presentation, use this feature when you save your presentation. This will save it in just the form that it appears on your personal computer. Far too often I have seen presentations with funny fonts, with the presenter apologizing saying "Gee, it didn't look this way on my office computer." This change occurs because the fonts available on one computer are not necessarily the same as those available on another. Because you'll never know what is available on the computer you'll be using for your presentation (unless you bring your own laptop), the "Pack and Go" feature can save a lot of embarrassment.

SUMMARY TABLE 1.4 Working with PowerPoint

Why you might want to use PowerPoint

- Hyperlinks are useful to move easily to Web sites
- Use of multimedia facilities is relatively easy with PowerPoint.

Working with PowerPoint Features

- Introduce text by paragraph points instead of all at once
- For the clearest displays, the best colors are black on white
- Repeat your current topic heading across multiple PowerPoint slides
- Do not use PowerPoint animations or sounds
- Display each data point on a graph sequentially with a mouse click
- Use the "pack and go" feature

Making graphs

Using graphs is probably the best way to display your data when giving a presentation. Done well, your graph can summarize a lot of information in a simple picture. "Doing it well," of course, is the catch. Below I outline a few suggestions that should get you started on the way to clear graph making. When reading through my suggestions, you should keep in mind some important suggestions made by Smithson (pp. 71–72) in his book on statistics.[4] Among other things, he reminds us to (1) "avoid distorting what the data have to say," (2) "present many numbers in a small space without clutter," (3) "make large data sets coherent," and (4) "graph data two or more times when needed." This last point suggests that you should try a variety of different visual representations of your data before you settle on a final one for your presentation. By making different types of graphs (e.g., using bar charts or line graphs; using or not using standard error bars) with the same data, you will learn what is the clearest and most straightforward way to present your particular data set.

Choosing graph types

My first piece of advice for choosing graph types is simple. Never use three-dimensional graphs for presenting two-dimensional data. Adding depth simply for flair rather than content actually makes the graphs more difficult to read accurately. I'll demonstrate this in Figure 1.1.

My second piece of advice is also simple: Never use pie charts. Pie charts give the impression that your data sum to 100 because the whole

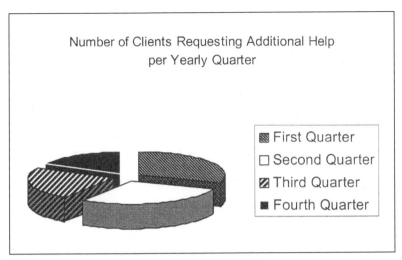

Number of Clients Requesting Additional Help
per Yearly Quarter

▨ First Quarter
☐ Second Quarter
▨ Third Quarter
■ Fourth Quarter

FIGURE 1.1. An example of the negative features of pie and three-dimensional charts. Don't use them! (Note: I made up these data for this example.)

pie is 100%; if your data do not sum to 100, then obviously you will be misleading your audience. Pie charts are also difficult to read, particularly when comparing across conditions or categories. Instead of pie charts, you should use bar charts, at least when you are presenting frequency data. Compare Figures 1.1 and 1.2 ,which present identical data. In Figure 1.1 it is difficult, if not impossible, to determine whether the first and

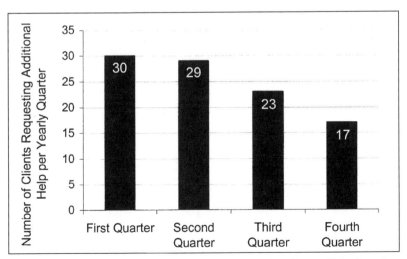

FIGURE 1.2. An example of the positive features of bar charts. (Note: I made up these data for this example.)

second quarters differ from each other. In Figure 1.2, however, the difference is clear with a simple glance (even without the numbers written in the bars). Moreover, Figure 1.1 implies a sum of 100; but a look at the values written in Figure 1.2 shows that the sum is actually 99.

My third piece of advice for choosing graph types applies when presenting statistical interactions. One of the first things beginning statistics students learn is that when graphed lines are not parallel, the data are characterized by an interaction. Given that most professionals in the behavioral sciences know this (and, in fact, this is precisely what the mathematics of interaction testing are evaluating), then presenting your data as lines will communicate your interactions (or absence of interactions) most clearly. So if you want to demonstrate an interaction or its absence, I recommend using line charts rather than bar charts. Of course, by following my advice, you can easily run into the problem of implying that your data are continuous across conditions when, in fact, they may not be. Thus make sure you emphasize to your audience the categorical rather than continuous nature of your experimental or predicting conditions if, in fact, this is the case!

Using colors and fill effects

I discussed colors earlier in this chapter under the topic of PowerPoint usage. All of what I said there applies to the making of graphs as well. The most critical point is that you should be using the greatest contrast possible, which turns out to be black and white. Note too that unless you have a color printer and a color photocopier, your overheads will be black and white by default; any colors will appear as shades of gray and will possibly be indistinguishable. If you insist on adding color to your overhead, slide, or PowerPoint graphs, then you should use it only on the lines or bars in the body of your graphs. All background should be white, and the graph itself and all labels should be black. The colored lines and bars representing your data will then be relatively salient. Again, use highly saturated reds and blues; pale tans, yellows, and grays will be very difficult for your audience to see.

When you use bar charts, you may want to use different patterned fill effects to differentiate one category (e.g., males) from another (e.g., females). This is particularly so if you will not be using colors to make this distinction. If you only have two categories, then solid black bars contrasted with solid white bars with black outlines will be the clearest for your audience. If you have three or more categories, then (1) start introducing simple hatch marks (e.g., //// or \\\\) as your fill effects, and (2) separate bars with hatch marks from each other by the solid black and solid white bars. You should realize that if you find yourself having more than, say, five different categories needing differentiation, the graph as a whole will become difficult to read no matter what you do; in this case, you should consider reducing the amount of information in your graph, perhaps by making two or more graphs.

Label your graphs in a clear and meaningful manner

Labeling your graphs in a clear and meaningful manner is one of the most important things you can do. If your graphs are poorly labeled, then all is lost from the beginning. Here are some basic tips. First, it is a convention to place your dependent or criterion variable on the y (vertical) axis, and one of your independent or predictor variables on the x (horizontal) axis. Because it is a convention, most of your audience will be expecting this; so if you do not follow this convention, you will lose your audience from the word go. If you have more than one independent or predictor variable, then embed these in the graph itself. I have displayed this (poorly) in Figure 1.3 and (well) in Figure 1.4. In these figures, the dependent variable is people's subjective evaluations (along the y axis); one independent variable is the experimental condition (along the x axis); and the second independent variable is gender (embedded in the graph itself). If you have more than two independent variables, then you should use more than one graph. Displaying three or more independent variables in the same graph can be very confusing.

All other aspects within your graph should be labeled. As an example of a bad line graph, Figure 1.3 has labels for neither the "series" nor the

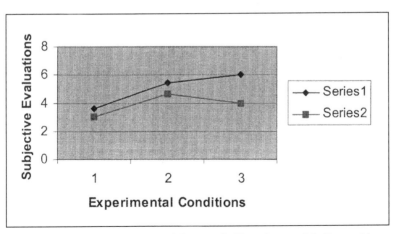

FIGURE 1.3. An example of a bad line graph. There is poor labeling and low contrast. (Note: I made up these data for this example.)

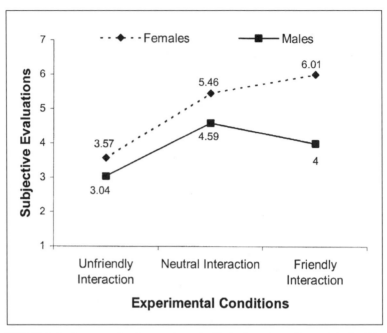

FIGURE 1.4. An example of a good graph. (Note: I made up these data for this example.)

"experimental conditions." Of course, you may explain this verbally during your presentation, but the information should also be written on your graph. In this respect, Figure 1.4 is much clearer. Notice that another difference between Figure 1.3 and Figure 1.4 is the size of the y axis. Although many computer graphics programs will have particular default values for your y axis, these may be completely meaningless in the context of your data. If I had measured people's subjective evaluations along a seven-point scale, then the values of zero and eight in Figure 1.3 have no meaning. If you use rating scales, my advice is to scale the y axis to the size of your rating scale; this will ensure that the y axis makes sense, while keeping you honest about the size of your effects!

One final point I should make pertains to the use of standard error bars. The use of these are conventions in some disciplines but not in others, although the trend across all disciplines is to use them. This definitely has the positive value of providing more information to your audience; you will not only be telling the central tendency (i.e., the mean) but the variability in your data as well. My advice for the use of these in professional presentations is mixed. If your audience is expecting these, then it's best to use them. I failed to do so during my first departmental presentation in my current job, and within minutes after I finished, two different colleagues were at my heels complaining that they could not understand my data without error bars. However, if your audience is not expecting them (e.g., if they are not standard in your discipline), then using error bars may end up providing more clutter than clarity on your graphs.

SUMMARY TABLE 1.5 Making graphs

- Using graphs is probably the best way to display your data
- Never use three-dimensional graphs to present two-dimensional data
- Use bar charts not pie charts
- Line graphs are good for displaying statistical interactions
- The best colors have the highest contrast (i.e., black and white)
- Label your graphs in a clear and meaningful manner
- Consider using standard error bars on your graphs

Using Handouts

Use handouts only when you have a lot of information

I have very little to say about using handouts during your professional presentation. Basically, my advice is *not* to use them. Handouts are very distracting. Distributing them takes time away from your presentation, and talking while distributing the handouts is just awful for you and your audience. Worse yet is that your audience will read your handouts while you are speaking, meaning that they will *not* be listening to what you have to say. If you want to make available a written report of your presentation after you have finished, fine. But do so *after*, not before or during. What you should do is present all relevant information to the audience verbally and via overheads and slides.

There are, however, two main situations when you should use handouts. The first (and definitely more important) is when you are presenting a lot of very complex information. Recall that I said *not* to clutter your overheads with too much information. But there will be times when presenting detailed information—lots of numbers, dates, figures, and so on—will be essential to your presentation. In such instances, you should use handouts. In doing so, your audience will be able to examine, study, and write on the information in a way that they could not otherwise. Of course, you will still need to guide your audience through the relevant information. Do not simply present pages of data, for example, and then say, "Well, you have all the information, so I'll just give you a minute or two to read it yourself." It is your job as the presenter to guide and inform your audience.

The second situation in which you may want to use handouts is if you are giving a presentation in which your audience has paid to see you. In these situations, the audience often wants something physical that they can take home with them. Again, however, you can easily make available a written report of your presentation when you are finished.

SUMMARY TABLE 1.6 Handouts

In general

- Do not use handouts

In specific cases, use handouts when

- You are presenting a lot of detailed information
- Your fee-paying audience is expecting them

Notes

1. See, for example, O'Shea, R. P. (2000). *Writing for psychology: An introductory guide for students* (3rd ed.). Sydney: Harcourt Australia; and Findlay, B. (2000). *How to write psychology laboratory reports and essays.* Frenchs Forest, N.S.W.: Pearson Education Australia.
2. Loftus, G. R. (1993). Editorial comment. *Memory & Cognition, 21*, 1–3; see also Loftus, G. R. (1993). A picture is worth a thousand *p* values: On the irrelevance of hypothesis testing in the microcomputer age. *Behavior Research Methods, Instruments, & Computers, 25*, 250–256.
3. Yager, D., Aquilante, K., & Plass, R. (1998). High and low luminance letters, acuity reserve, and font effects on reading speed. *Vision Research, 38*, 2527–2531.
4. Smithson, M. (2000). *Statistics with confidence.* London: Sage. This is a good source to help you with graph making. Several of the points I make in this section have been adopted from his book.

Chapter 2

Delivery
Presenting your work

Before beginning

Make sure you have practiced out loud

As I said in chapter 1, you *must* practice your full presentation multiple times, out loud, with an overhead, slide, or PowerPoint projector. This is an absolute necessity. One thing I can be confident in promising you is that your presentation will fail if you fail to practice.

Arrive on time

You might find this to be a point not worth mentioning, but it is absolutely essential that you arrive to your presentation venue on time. Although I have never been late, I have been on the waiting end of a late speaker. It is very embarrassing and nerve-racking for your host and highly unprofessional for you (even if you don't get embarrassed at such things). Make sure you allow enough travel time to get lost, for your car to break down, to get caught in traffic, or to have a delayed flight. All these things (and more) can and do happen. Remember that one of your goals in giving professional presentations is correct impression management (see "The right goals" in chapter 1). It doesn't matter how brilliant you are, arriving late starts you off on the wrong foot. Some of your audience will have left, so they'll never know how brilliant you are, and some will be in a bad mood, so they'll be less receptive to your message (see "Humor" in chapter 4).

Bring overhead pens or a pointer to your presentation

In addition to your overheads, slides, or PowerPoint display, you should bring with you to your presentation some overhead pens or a pointer of some form (pocket-sized laser pointers are readily available and quite inexpensive now). The purpose of the pens and pointers is to emphasize specific aspects of your presentation to your audience and to clarify certain aspects if questions have been asked. With the pens, however, under no circumstance should you be writing *new* information on your overheads. All of the information should be written on your overheads prior to arriving at your venue.

There are two instances when writing information on your overheads is appropriate. The first is when an audience member wants clarification of some sort. In this instance, it will often help if you simply underline, circle, or place an arrow next to the point that has already been written on your overhead. You might say something like, "Oh, I understand. You were confusing this point here that I've circled in red with this other point that I've circled in blue. I can see how they appear similar, but notice this important difference. . . . " And then you provide a verbal explanation. The second instance when you might want to use an overhead pen is to emphasize a particular point. In this case, before the audience members get confused and ask questions, you might say, "I want to make sure this is very clear. Notice how this second point I am making, which I have now circled in red, is different in important ways from the first, which I have circled in blue." This strategy is good, but it can also backfire if you are feeling anxious; feeling anxious sometimes makes people lose their concentration and circle or otherwise mark the wrong place on the overhead or, worse yet, makes them lose track of the entire point they are trying to make. The best strategy would be to circle the two points—or highlight them in some other manner—*prior* to arriving at your venue (i.e., while you are in your office making your overheads). In this manner, the points would already be emphasized before your anxiety began.

Obviously, if you use slides or PowerPoint, then the pens will have no purpose. But you still may want to use a pointer of some sort. In this way, you can point directly to the topic on the projection that you want your audience to attend to without jumping up and down like a fool trying to reach the written topic. Of course, you can also use the pointer if you use overheads, but with these you can simply use your finger (or a pen) to point directly at the overhead on the projector, and the shadow will be projected on the screen.

Check your equipment before you start

I said earlier in this chapter that you should ensure you arrive on time. Actually, you should always arrive a bit early to your venue and check all of the equipment you will use before you start your presentation. Ensure that the projectors you will use actually project onto the screen and that the projection can be seen throughout the room. Also ensure that the projections are in focus. Far too many times, speakers begin their presentations looking at the audience (as they should) and placing an overhead on the projector with no knowledge that it is being projected out of focus or on the ceiling! Of course, it is your host's responsibility to provide you with proper equipment in good working condition. But do not rely on it. Check everything before you begin. If you notice something is wrong, ask your host to fix it immediately. At our university, for example, our weekly professional presentations are given in an open lecture room used by a variety of departments. The university management, in all its wisdom, decided that it would permanently supply a slide projector in the room, but no lens; lenses are up to each department. The first time we found this out is when our presenter arrived early and checked out the equipment. It was the presenter who informed us (the hosts) of our own unprofessionalism. Luckily, he did so with enough time prior to the beginning of the presentation to allow us to find a lens.

Note the time you begin and when you have to end

In chapter 1, I said that you must write your presentation to your time limit. This is essential. However, even though you have written to your time limit and have practiced your presentation multiple times out loud, you still must keep track of your time. You will be surprised how much time is taken up by your introduction and a few clarification questions here and there from your audience. So note the exact time when you began your presentation. If you are like me, write it down on a small piece of paper or directly on your presentation notes; otherwise, with all the other things you have to attend to, and all the anxiety, you'll forget. Don't stop there, however. Note also when you have to finish, and write this time down too. This way, you can keep track of the time *easily*, without having to calculate every ten minutes. The one thing you should definitely not do is ask your hosts to keep track of the time for you. This will simply distract them from what you have to say, it will distract your audience, and it will distract you (see also the section "Watch the time" later in this chapter).

Speaking to people

You finally made it! This is what it is all about: speaking to people. In this section, I outline some tips that should help you make a more successful professional presentation when you are actually up there in front of your audience.

Face your audience

Advising you to face your audience may sound a bit pedantic. I can assure you, however, that this is surprisingly overlooked by many professional speakers. Below are three pitfalls commonly encountered by speakers.

Pitfall 1: Speaking to your notes

Speakers who have not practiced their presentations often speak to their notes instead of to the audience. This comes about because the presenters are simply reading and do not want to take their eyes off the notes for fear of getting lost. But by speaking to their notes, something else gets lost: their audience. And so will yours. Because you will not be making eye contact with your audience, you will not be engaging them as much as you ought. You will then be running the risk of them not making eye contact with you and, instead, staring out the window, inspecting their thumbs, or reading the book they brought along in case it was a boring presentation. When you have practiced, however, you can afford to divert your eyes from your notes and direct them, instead, to your audience. By looking at your audience—the whole audience, not just one or two people—you will be better able to maintain the attention you deserve from that audience.

Pitfall 2: Speaking to your overheads, slides, or PowerPoint display

The second pitfall people often encounter when not speaking to their audience is either staring at the overheads sitting on the projector or, worse yet, facing the projection screen instead of the audience (indeed, their back is actually to the audience). When facing the overheads, you will face the same problems as when reading from your notes. When facing the projection screen, life is even worse. Not only will you fail to engage your audience, but your audience will have difficulty hearing you because you will be speaking away from them. Although I advise you later in this chapter always to check the projection screen after presenting each new overhead or slide, make sure you turn back around again to face the audience. If you want to point out specific aspects of the overhead or slide, stand at an angle, with your side to the audience, so you can turn your head to look at the screen but then can easily turn back to face your audience. And if you are using overheads, do not face the screen at all; continue facing the audience, but point directly at the overhead slide on the projector—and look up while you speak!

Pitfall 3: Speaking to an imaginary audience

This final pitfall is actually a catchall for all those other places speakers look other than at their audience. This might be at the ceiling, at the floor, at their hands, or out the window. You can be sure that when you are looking at these, your audience will be looking elsewhere too—maybe out the window with you! So face your audience.

Project your voice

Remember that you will be speaking to your audience under the assumption that they will be listening to you. But they will never listen if they cannot hear. I have seen far too many intelligent speakers fail to get their messages across because they are speaking so no one can hear them. The most common problem is that speakers project their voices no more than they do when they are in an interpersonal conversation. When you are just chatting with a single friend, then a soft tone of voice is all that's needed; it's polite. However, when speaking to an audience, this type of interpersonal approach to the loudness of your voice is insufficient. You must speak so that each and every person in the audience can hear you. And it does not matter if this soft, interpersonal speech is "just your style." When you are up in front of an audience, you are there to be heard. So do not put the burden on your audience to maintain an absolutely silent lecture theater. People will naturally cough, shuffle their feet or some papers, or even whisper to each other; the fan of your overhead or slide projector will make noise; outside passersby or cars will add further noise. You will be competing with all of this. Do not be rude and make people strain or move; speak up and be heard.

Speak to the people in the back row

The farther away from you that people sit, the more difficulty they will have in hearing you, and the more you will have to work to ensure they do hear you. The most simple strategy is for you to speak loudly enough so that the people in the back row can hear you. Do not speak only to the folks in the front row. Of course, accomplishing this task of speaking to the people "in the cheap seats" in the back sometimes means speaking as if you are shouting. Hopefully, you will have access to microphones if the lecture theater is that large. Nevertheless, there may not be a microphone, and you will have to project your voice as you do your visual aids, in a manner that is accessible to every person in the audience. Again, it does not matter if you are naturally soft-spoken and your "nature" does not allow you to speak that loud. You must speak up anyway. If people cannot hear you, then you might as well not be there.

Ask if the audience can hear you

The most important thing you should do is simply ask your audience if they can hear you. This is very reasonable and will show your audience your genuine concern for them. Make sure you ask, of course, at the very beginning of your presentation. If you ask midway through, you may have already lost half of your audience.

Use microphones

The easiest way to ensure your audience can hear you is to use a microphone. Of course, not every venue you will be in will have microphone facilities. But if the one you are in does have them, use them. Note, however, that one of the biggest problems that people often have with microphones is that they are not used to hearing their voices projected so loudly, and they get self-conscious and their anxiety increases. Don't let this happen to you. Initially, you will need to attend to the speakers, just to make sure they are not too loud, too soft, have static, or feedback. But once you and your audience are satisfied, ignore the speakers and attend to your head.

Speak from your overheads, slides, or PowerPoint displays

In chapter 1 (sections "Making overheads and slides" and "Working with PowerPoint"), I spent a lot of time describing how to make your overheads, slides, or PowerPoint displays. My advice in using them is based on simple practicalities. These visual aids not only will help your audience follow what you are saying, but they will help you say what you want to in the first place (see "What you should do: Lecture from overheads, slides, and PowerPoint displays" in chapter 1). Your overheads, slides, or PowerPoint displays will serve as your notes. By the time it actually comes to present your work, you will have already spent a great deal of time on your presentation, including your visual aids. This will ensure that the presentation itself is logical and clear. You should use the points on your visual aids as cues to what you will say next. In essence, you should be presenting your audience with a few key words on your visual aids, and then filling in the blanks with your verbal explanations. Your prepared overheads, slides, or PowerPoint displays will ensure you will progress in the correct and logical order, and they will ensure that you will speak on each topic that you wanted to. If you've prepared them correctly, you can put your complete faith in your visual aids, so you never have to worry about missing a point or presenting your ideas out of order.

Do not read word for word (unless you freeze up)

As I said earlier, I highly recommend that you do *not* read your presentation, but rely on your overheads, slides, or PowerPoint displays instead. Reading nearly always bores the audience. When reading, you are most likely to encounter one of at least three problems. The first problem people encounter when reading is that they speak in a monotone. They use no vocal intonations at all—possibly because they are concentrating so hard on reading—and it comes out sounding like a drone. In the end, this is really boring to listen to. The second problem people encounter when reading is just the opposite; this is when people read with overly dramatic vocal intonations. When this happens, it isn't boring, but it is silly, and these people end up looking—and sounding—foolish. Finally, the third problem with reading is that people speak too quickly, failing to pause at appropriate places such as at commas and periods. The presenters, as readers, can, of course, see the commas and periods, so they are able to understand the text. The audience, however, is not privy to this information, and the presentation ends up sounding more like an endless string of words than meaningful text.

So instead of reading, use your overheads, slides, or PowerPoint displays as prompts. Having a complete set of visual aids from which you can speak—and practicing your presentation multiple times out loud with these aids—will provide you with sufficient information and expertise to complete your presentation successfully. And although I have repeatedly said not to speak extemporaneously, you should speak *as if* your presentation is extemporaneous. This will come with practice; your goal is to speak knowledgeably and clearly—with your visual aids as prompts—while overcoming the reading problems I've just outlined.

There is only one time when I would condone reading your presentation word for word. This is when your anxiety is so great that you freeze. When you can't speak for your fear, then by all means, read your presentation. You'll be up there and your audience will be waiting, so you'll need to do something. And if it's reading, then read. I hasten to point out, of course, that my whole purpose in writing this book is to provide you with enough advice to allow you to be sufficiently prepared so that your anxiety will *not* overwhelm you. If you do, indeed, follow the advice in this book, then you should be prepared enough to go through with your presentation with minimum anxiety and not be forced to read.

Do not speak extemporaneously

In chapter 1 (section "Writing pitfall 1") I made a strong point in telling you not to speak extemporaneously. I want to reiterate that point here when writing about actually speaking your presentation. It is often tempting to move slightly off your prepared presentation when a new idea hits you or when audience members interrupt with questions. As I said earlier, however, moving off your prepared presentation is fraught with problems. In the first instance, you may find yourself sidetracking and telling a story that you did not intend to. This will only confuse you and your audience, as you diverge from your original topic. Secondly, if you are moving in the direction of questions from your audience, you are likely to end up talking about the audience's chosen topic, not yours. And as I discuss in chapter 3, in the section titled "Maintain control over your audience," this is not good. Your audience has come to see you, to hear what you have to say, to learn what contributions you have made to your profession. Remember, you will have gone to a great deal of trouble to prepare and perfect your presentation. Stick to it. Do not be seduced into sidetracking and extemporaneously speaking about ideas that pop into your head or that are forced upon you by your audience.

Avoid writing new information on your overheads (or blackboards)

Earlier in this chapter, I told you to bring pens to your presentation in case you need to highlight something specific while you're talking. But I also said that you actually should do your highlighting *prior* to actually giving your presentation. You should avoid writing new information on your overheads (or a blackboard if there is one) in the middle of your presentation. Writing new information is bad for at least two reasons. First, as I said above, it can make you easily lose your train of thought. By shifting your attention from speaking to your audience to finding your pen or chalk, finding the location at which you want to write, and actually writing, you can easily forget what you wanted to say. Second, writing information simply wastes time. While you're standing there writing new information, your audience is patiently waiting. But why? Why should you make your audience sit there in polite and sometimes painful silence while you do work that you should have done prior to your arrival? There's no good answer, because you shouldn't. All information that you want displayed to your audience on your overheads (or slides) should be written on them prior to your arrival. Don't put yourself in a situation where you can lose your place and where your audience must endure painful silences.

Read your overheads

Earlier I said not to read your presentation word for word. However, it is essential that you *do* read all of the text you put up on your overheads and slides (remember, these should only have short points). It is not sufficient to put up text and expect your audience to read it themselves. Your job is to read it to them. As presenter, you are the one who has to do the work, not the audience. The overheads and slides are simply *aids* for your audience; they are not supplements for your speaking. Far too many times presenters say, "Well, here's really what I want to conclude, so you can just read it yourself." This is a cop-out. By making the audience do the work, presenters are really shifting the burden of the presentation from themselves to their audience, and that's not good. These presenters fail to realize that if audience members wanted to *read* their work, the audience members wouldn't have come to this oral presentation in the first place. Moreover, these presenters are expecting the audience to attend to and process two sources of different information at once: the information being spoken and the information being displayed. This is far too much to ask from your audience and, frankly, is far too confusing. Your audience will be expecting you to talk about what you've displayed. The simple lesson is: Read your overheads.

Do not display text without reading it or referring to it

In the last section, I said that it is essential for you to read the text you put on your overheads and slides. The point here is a closely aligned one, but one often overlooked by presenters. Sometimes presenters will use, for example, figures or graphs with lots of information on them, such as axis labeling, source of the data, and so on. Or sometimes presenters will re-use overheads or slides from previous presentations. In either case (and others like them), in their current presentation, presenters may only be interested in a subset of the information displayed. Unfortunately, your audience will not know this. Any text you display, your audience will read. And if you do not mention specific text you've displayed, your audience will be left in the dark as to its meaning. They will naturally assume, simply because you've displayed the information, that the information is important. But if you do not speak to this information, you will only confuse your audience; they will be wondering whether they actually missed something (possibly when they were reading the text while you were speaking). So do not display text on your overheads, slides, or PowerPoint displays without reading it or referring to it. If you do not want to read or refer to the text, then do not put it on your visual aids in the first place.

Look at the screen each time you display a new overhead or slide

Things can go wrong, and they will go wrong if you're not vigilant. Although you will have checked that the projector was in focus and on the screen before you began your presentation, problems still may arise. Sometimes parts of the old overhead projector you're using will slowly slip out of alignment; sometimes the overhead you made is too big for the screen, so the audience cannot see all of it; sometimes you'll have mistakenly placed a slide in upside down. Whatever the case, you should look at the projection screen each time you display a new overhead or slide. In this way, you will always know exactly what the audience sees. If there is a problem, you'll be able to fix it without fuss; if there's no problem, all the better. In any event, a quick glance over your shoulder will save you time and embarrassment and will ensure that your audience will continue to follow you.

Reveal the information on your overheads, slides, and PowerPoint displays slowly

When presenting your overheads, slides, and PowerPoint displays, reveal your information slowly. It won't take you very long to learn that whatever you display, your audience will read. And if you display a lot of information, they will read that information *without listening to what you have to say about it!* So the common approach of displaying an overhead or slide with the next, say, five points that you want to make, and then working your way through each point one by one is not necessarily the best approach. I can assure you that while you're talking about point one, your audience will be reading about points two through five. And they won't be listening to you. You can't fault your audience for this. They have every reason to expect that you've displayed information for them to read, and so they read it. What you have to do, instead, is actively take charge of your audience's reading. If you want them to read all five points, then display them all. But if you want them only to read the one point about which you are currently speaking, then reveal that one point only. Typically, it's this latter situation that most presenters want.

There are two basic ways of displaying your information slowly. The first way you can use when you are displaying overheads. Simply place your overhead on the projector, and then cover up all unwanted text with a sheet of paper. Because your overheads will be in a structured format (see "Keep your overheads, slides, and PowerPoint displays in a structured format" in chapter 1), you can simply slide the covering paper down the overhead at each step of the way, revealing each point as you make it. If you use PowerPoint, then you can display each point only after each new mouse click (see "Introducing text systematically" in chapter 1). The second way to display your information slowly is simply to put on your visual aids (i.e., overheads, slides, and PowerPoint displays) only that information that you want to talk about at any given time. As you move from point to point, you change overheads or slides. Possibly *at the end*, you can have a summary overhead or slide displaying all the points you just made to help your audience integrate the information. The choice of either of these two ways of revealing information is up to you. The positive feature of the first method over the second is that you use relatively fewer resources (e.g., you make one overhead instead of five). The positive feature of the second method over the first is that your audience will not get the impression that you are hiding information from them when you cover your overheads; this does actually annoy some people.

Do not speak on one topic while expecting the audience to read another

As I said earlier in this chapter, it is essential to read all information you present on your overheads and slides. It's worth reiterating here. A common mistake that presenters make when displaying their overheads or slides is to display one set of text, but speak about something else. This happens at times when, for example, the presenter displays what he or she thinks is a meaningful or enlightened quotation. The quotation is displayed and is there in the background (figuratively and literally), hopefully sparking some sort of interest in the audience. I can assure you, however, that this is an awful strategy. As I said before, audience members will be trying to read your text and won't be listening to what you have to say. When your audience has finally finished the text and can now listen to you, they'll realize that you're speaking about something different. Remember, as presenter you *cannot* ask your audience to do your work for you. It is your responsibility to draw all connections between ideas. This includes, for example, the connections between that enlightened quotation in the background and the content of your verbal presentation. Simply put, do not speak on one topic while expecting the audience to read another. It is far too confusing for audience members and will only distract and frustrate them. If you display information, talk about it.

Explain rather than tell

One mistake speakers often make in their professional presentations is to tell the audience information rather than explaining it. What do I mean by this? Telling is simply stating—stating the facts, stating the methods, stating the figures, and so on. This may be satisfactory for people as knowledgeable in your specialty area as you are. However, you are probably the only one with that degree of knowledge. So you will have to do more than simply tell; you will have to elucidate, develop, elaborate, and generally make what you have to say understandable to everyone. You must explain. And you must do so step-by-step.

Assume your audience is unsophisticated

Okay, now you are probably a bit confused. In chapter 1, I said that you should assume sophistication in your audience. Now I'm saying just the opposite. I can assure you, I am not trying to confuse you. The goal is really more to provide topic-dependent advice. My advice previously was that you should assume some degree of shared knowledge between yourself and your audience. Now I am saying that upon recognizing potentially shared knowledge, you should work from the premise that your audience is completely naïve to your ideas and general topic area. Making this new, secondary assumption will allow you to prepare your presentation in an explanatory way, going into just a bit more detail and following a logical, step-by-step description of what your work is about. You will be prepared to spend a bit more time on the novel contributions that you have made, ensuring that all audience members will be able to follow what you have to say. Again, this doesn't negate what I said earlier; if there is a research method, for example, that has been around for 20 years and that most people in the audience have used, do not explain it. But if you have made new contributions (as you hopefully will have), do not assume your audience will know them or understand them as well as you do. For many, if not all, audience members, your presentation of your new contributions will be the first time they will have heard them, so you must explain them in as much detail as time will permit.

Meet the audience

In most cases, you will be provided with a lectern or podium of some nature when giving your professional presentation. It is very common—and very reasonable—for speakers to stand behind this podium for the duration of the presentation and to place their notes, overheads, pens, and other implements on it. But sometimes, nervous speakers use the podium to hide from their audience. They use it as some sort of barrier between them and what they perceive as potential threats. And behind the podium, they can fidget their hands and feet nervously without being seen. If you are a very nervous speaker, or if you are a novice and are concerned with losing your notes, then definitely spend your time behind the podium. However, this strategy may have a drawback. Standing behind the podium leads many speakers to adopt stiff and rigid body postures. Given that your audience is present to hear what you have to say and not how you look when you say it, there is nothing really wrong with this posture. However, it does have the negative consequence of making you a boring visual stimulus, a rigid "talking head." If you are feeling confident, then I recommend walking *in front* of the podium at least once. Meet your audience. The best times to do this are at the very beginning and the very end of your presentation. At the beginning, you can introduce yourself and your general topic in a casual and engaging way (see "What you should do: Tell a story" in chapter 1). At the end, you can summarize your presentation in an intuitive, conversational manner. In either case, meeting your audience brings you to them, increases your chances of engaging their attention, and makes you more like someone they can understand and identify with (see "The importance of shared group membership" in chapter 4). All of this will help bring your message to them.

Watch the time

I have said repeatedly that you must speak to your time limit. And earlier in this chapter, I said to note the time you begin and when you have to end. Noting the time, however, is not just something you do at the beginning of your presentation; it continues throughout it. So keep your eye on the clock. Speaking too long or too short can be problematic (see "Write to your time limit" in chapter 1). If you've practiced your talk prior to your presentation, then you should have no problems. However, during the real thing, you could find yourself going a bit fast or a bit slow. If you find yourself not keeping to your time schedule, *you should be willing to cut things if you seem to be going over your time limit, or to slow your pace if you seem to be going under your time limit.* The latter is less likely to happen if you have practiced your presentation ahead of time. The former, however, is more likely, especially if you've had a long introduction or lots of questions. If this happens, you must be willing to sacrifice some of your presentation. Of course, you do not want to end the presentation without getting to your main point. So you must keep track of your time (see also

---

SUMMARY TABLE 2.2 Speaking to people

What you should do

- Face your audience
- Speak to the people in the back row
- Ask if the audience can hear you
- Use microphones
- Reveal your overheads slowly
- Read your overheads
- Look at the screen each time you display a new overhead or slide
- Assume your audience is unsophisticated to your specialty
- Meet the audience
- Explain rather than tell
- Watch the time

What you should not do

- Do not speak to your notes
- Do not speak to your overheads or slides
- Do not speak to an imaginary audience
- Do not read word-for-word (unless you freeze up)
- Do not speak extemporaneously
- Avoid writing new information on your overheads (or blackboards)
- Do not display text without reading it or referring to it
- Do not speak on one topic while expecting the audience to read another

chapter 3, "Maintain control over your audience"). If you notice early on that you're a little behind schedule, then you can, for example, give briefer reviews of the previous literature, or of your methods, or even skip some of your data. These decisions you'll have to make "on the go," and they will require particular attention and concentration not to get lost. Again, this should not happen if you've practiced your presentation. One way to limit your extemporaneous decision is to decide *ahead of time* what you will cut during your actual presentation if you find yourself in need to do so. Of course, the things you cut can be revisited during the question period if your audience asks for clarification or further information.

Stage fright

As I said in the introduction, fear of public speaking is commonly experienced by people in our culture. People fear looking foolish, appearing as if they don't know what they're talking about; they (we!) fear others criticizing them; and they fear people not liking their own work and that of others in their profession. For a professional presenter, this is stage fright. The first thing you should know is that a little anxiety often helps motivate people to perform better; the world was never meant to be anxiety free. The second thing you should know is that all speakers, even the good ones, have these fears; don't believe otherwise. And the third thing you should know is that the good speakers are good only because of hard work, practice, and experience; with these, you will be a good speaker too. Remember, the whole point of this book is to help you give a good professional presentation—to help you prepare your presentation (and yourself) so that it *is* good, and so that you *won't* look foolish. If you follow the advice in this book, you should be sufficiently prepared to realize that your fears are unjustified. You won't look like a fool; in fact, with experience, you'll "wow" your audience.

But what happens if your audience is particularly critical? What happens if they are rude and interrupt? I answer these questions in greater detail in the next chapter, "Defense: Answering questions and defending your work." However, there are two points that I will emphasize here. First, it is essential to maintain control over your audience. How do you do this? Never accept rude audience members, and never accept interruptions. Of course, sometimes an audience member may want clarification on a specific point you've made; that's fine. But other interruptions that change your topic, suggest that you should be talking about something else, or ones that trivialize what you're saying are unacceptable. Don't stand for these, and don't assume that the rude questioner has the right simply because he or she is in the audience or because he or she is of higher status than you. Rudeness is unacceptable by anyone. The second point I want to emphasize is that, as I've said before, you must practice your full presentation multiple times, out loud, with an overhead, slide, or PowerPoint projector. You may be sick of me saying this. However, this is truly the best way for you to give a good presentation. And it is the best way for you to reduce your stage fright. If you've practiced, you'll know what to say, you'll know how to say it, and you'll know that you know these. You'll have the skills, abilities, and confidence to give a good professional presentation.

SUMMARY TABLE 2.3 Stage fright

- Maintain control over your audience
- Practice your full presentation multiple times, out loud, with an overhead, slide, or PowerPoint projector

Chapter 3

Defense
Answering questions and defending your work

Anticipate questions before your presentation

I have repeatedly emphasized throughout this book that you should *not* speak extemporaneously and that all your work should be done *before* you arrive to give your presentation. When your audience asks questions, however, the ball game changes; you must speak extemporaneously. And if you're anxious, inexperienced, or unprepared, this could easily be a problem. It's not, however, without remedy. Like everything else, you can begin your work back at your office, before arriving at your presentation venue. To do this, you must *anticipate* questions, comments, criticisms, and (unfortunately) nonsequiturs that your audience may pose to you. I'm under no illusions about this suggestion. It is hard work.

In anticipation, the first thing you should do is to learn about your audience. Who will be listening to you? Does your audience have particular biases or ways of approaching your topic? Are there members of the audience who seem to be chronically annoying to presenters? Answers to these and other similar questions necessitate homework, but there are many ways to learn who will be in your audience. Asking the person who invited you to speak is the easiest. I recall one head of a department in which I was once presenting who warned me ahead of time of another professor who was, effectively, chronically rude to presenters. This warning put me at ease when I looked in the back row during my presentation to see the accused professor snickering and chatting with his neighbors as I spoke. But it's not just rude people you should be interested in. What you want to know is the types of genuine questions typically asked by your audience. If you can't ask someone in order to ascertain this, then, depending on where you're speaking, you can (1) read a conference program of other speakers to see who may attend your presentation, (2) read a prospectus of the department you're speaking to, or (3) read a list of previous speakers to know who your audience is interested in. No matter what, knowing a little about your audience will help you anticipate the questions they'll ask.

When you find out about your audience, spend some time placing yourself in their seats. Try to view your presentation from their perspective. Of course, you must go farther than just thinking of their questions. You must try to answer them, and this is the really difficult part. Don't think you'll come up with an answer when you're up in front of the audience. You'll be too nervous for that. And don't think the audience won't ask the hard questions. They will. So spend time before you arrive at your presentation venue thinking about how you will respond to alternative explanations and criticisms of your work. Your time invested will reap large returns.

The second thing you should do when anticipating questions and comments is to ask one or more of your own colleagues *their* opinions about your work. Ask them to play devil's advocate and pose the difficult questions to you. Most colleagues will be willing to do this, so don't be shy. Most colleagues, however, will also try to be gentle to you, so watch out. You want colleagues who are as tough as possible; they should not be nice. Otherwise they could be leading you into a false sense of security. To help you best prepare, they must pose the difficult questions. And you must answer them.

Listen to your audience

When you're in the "thick of it," when your audience is asking questions and making comments, the most important thing you can do is *listen*. I'm convinced that most presenters don't actually listen to the questions posed because they often do not actually answer—or even address—the questions. I'm afraid that presenters believe either that the audience members have nothing of value to say or that the audience members will automatically be opposed to the thesis presented. No doubt some audience members really don't add anything of value, and some are in opposition. However, most audience members aren't fools; most are professionals like yourself and honestly attend your presentation to hear what you have to say. Because of this, most will have something of value to say, and will not be overly contentious. You must approach your audiences with this in mind. The best presenters actively attend to the questions and comments made by their audience members (even the rude ones) and address the comments and questions directly. The more you pay attention, the clearer your understanding of what they are asking will be, and the better able you will be to respond.

Repeat questions and comments

One simple way you can assure that you listen fully to your audience is by repeating the questions and comments made by them. By restating the question or comment, you can assure that: (1) you understand what was asked, and (2) the audience member asking the question or making the comment knows that you understand. Now, of course, simply repeating the question or comment as if mimicking will make you look a bit foolish. There is, fortunately, another reason for you to repeat the question or comment: Other audience members are likely not to have heard what was put to you. Audience members do not have the same responsibility that you do to speak loudly enough for all to hear. So, for example, a soft-spoken person in the front row may ask you a question that only you can really hear. Out of politeness to the rest of the audience, you should repeat this question. Basically, look at the person asking the question (or making the comment), attend to what he or she is saying, and when he or she is finished, look up to the rest of the audience and say something like, "In case some of you were not able to hear, I was asked to clarify how I gathered my sample of participants. This, of course, is a good question." And then answer the question if appropriate. (I will explain this further later in this chapter.)

Spend time thinking about what the audience says

When an audience member asks you a question, spend some time actually thinking about it. It's okay if you take a short pause to think before responding. A simple comment to your audience that you are thinking will make your silence understood. Although some presenters are afraid that not answering immediately may make them appear uninformed, this is not true. You will appear more uninformed if you answer without thinking. Immediately answering without thinking could easily lead you to answer the wrong question (one that wasn't really posed) or simply to say gibberish. So pause and think. Maybe on reflection, you'll realize that the question is one that you anticipated prior to your presentation. If so, great; you'll be able to answer easily and confidently. If not, then this pause must substitute for the preparations you made for all the rest of your presentation. Think about what was asked, and ask yourself some preliminary questions about the question itself. Is the audience member asking for clarification or offering alternative explanations of your findings? Did you actually speak to this issue in your presentation? Is the question actually pertinent to your topic? Don't immediately assume that the question is hostile or one that assumes you're somehow wrong in what you've said. By considering the nature of the question posed to you, you'll be able to provide the best answer possible. Most questions are honest, and most audience members really want to engage you in a discussion of your work. In fact, many audience members think it only *polite* to ask you questions. Having a presenter leave with no questions may send a message that the presentation was actually bad.

Be ready to accept that the audience may be right

Sometimes audience members will raise points in regard to your presentation about issues you have not considered. They may actually even suggest that what you've said is wrong. At times like this, many speakers have the tendency to get defensive, arguing that they are correct no matter what. If a debate ensues, and if you *are* wrong, then you will look foolish. So as I said above, pause and think about what you're being asked. And consider the possibility that any criticisms levied against you are correct. If they are, admit it. It is okay to make mistakes; it is okay to be wrong. If you think an audience member said something meaningful that suggests you've been mistaken, engage him or her in a conversation. Don't be defensive. Ask for further clarification. Ask how the ideas pertain to different aspects of what you've said. If the discussion becomes too complex, suggest you chat with the audience member after the entire presentation. In the end, the ideas may improve your work. Of course, you want to do as much work as possible *before* you arrive to your presentation to ensure that you *are* correct. But with each new presentation, you'll encounter new ideas, perspectives, and knowledge. Treat your presentations as a chance for you to learn from others as much as for you to inform them.

Maintain control over your audience

My previous advice was to listen to your audience members and be prepared to be wrong—if they're right! This is important. Most of the time, your audience will have meaningful input to your work. Most of the time, your audience will be genuine in asking questions and making comments. However, there are those unfortunate occasions when etiquette and professionalism seem to elude people. And this is why it is essential for you to maintain control over your audience. This may sound a bit draconian, but you must be in complete control for your entire presentation. Audience members—even genuine ones—may interrupt, ask questions, and make comments that ultimately move the presentation onto a topic on which you never intended to speak (see the section in chapter 1, "Writing pitfall 1" and in chapter 2, "Do not speak extemporaneously"). And because you never intended to speak on the topic, you didn't put it in your notes, you didn't practice ahead of time, and you will be unprepared and at their mercy. Moreover, you will be taking precious time away from what you did come to talk about. For any speaker, this could spell disaster. So don't be fooled. This type of audience behavior is plain old-fashioned rude and unprofessional, and you should never stand for it. It is unacceptable. Unfortunately, however, it is likely to happen to you sometime during your professional career; it has happened to me several times. But the audience members who do this are clearly not present to hear what you have to say. They are there either to have their own a priori views confirmed or because they would rather present their views from the relative security of a seat in the audience.

Do not accept impolite audience members

Impoliteness comes in many forms. It's not just typical rude comments. In my first professional job, for example, I had audience members who appeared to be genuinely concerned with the topic I was presenting, but who succeeded in steering my entire presentation in a completely different direction than I had planned. As a novice professional and a novice speaker, this spelled disaster for me. When audience members do this, even with a smile, they are rude. When you find yourself in a situation with a rude audience member taking you in directions you don't want to go, then simply say something like the following:

> These are all very interesting ideas, but I have come here today to present the ideas I've been working on over the past year. I have these ideas organized here in my presentation, and I would like to spend the remainder of my time presenting my prepared work. Possibly after the presentation, we can chat about your different ideas in your office.

In this way, you will have made it very clear that you have come prepared to talk about one particular thing and that you will continue talking about it independently of the audience member's preference. But what if the audience member says that nothing you can say will be of value until you settle the issue he or she has raised? If this happens, you do have to think a bit on your feet (remember, pause and think about the questions raised). In most cases, the audience member's assertion will simply be wrong. When this happens, say so and continue on with your prepared presentation. However, if the audience member is correct, you will have a bit more of a problem. The problem arises because you still want to present the work you prepared. Remember, speaking extemporaneously is problematic. So the best way out is to acknowledge the audience member's ideas but continue with your presentation anyway, saying something like the following.

> I see your point, and I can see how what you are saying may bring into question some of my conclusions. However, I'd still like to work through the entire presentation I prepared today. Then, after you have seen the entire picture, we can chat a bit more about it during the question-and-answer period.

Of course, the best way out of a situation like this last one is never to enter it in the first place. This means that you should always go into professional presentations with the best possible work you can achieve. Having a hostile audience member identify problems with your work in front of a lot of people is definitely the wrong time to find out about them!

Do not accept interruptions

Rude audience members should not be allowed to interrupt you in the first place. I often politely say at the beginning of my presentations that I have a lot of ideas I want to present to the audience and that I would like to do so without people asking questions in the middle. Of course, simple clarification questions are always accepted, and more detailed questions are always welcome at the end of the presentation. Simply announcing at the beginning of your presentation that you do not want interruptions, however, is often enough to fend off rude audience members. If the rude audience member *insists* on interrupting, simply say, "As I said at the beginning, I have a lot to talk about today, so I'd like to hold off on that question until the end."

Do not invite interruptions

Not only have I seen people invite interruptions from the audience, but I have done so myself. Only calamity follows. Never invite interruptions. I understand the desire to do so, especially if you want to maintain a relatively relaxed atmosphere and especially if you genuinely want feedback on your work. Don't do it anyway. The likelihood is that you will be taken in directions you do not want to go, you will not get a chance to finish what you came to say, and the presentation will fail. It definitely failed for me when I invited interruptions. And to top it off, you will have no one to blame but yourself for inviting people to interrupt. If you want feedback on your work, tell this to your audience, but tell them that you would like it during the question-and-answer period or later in separate meetings with them. In the end, a 50-minute or less professional presentation is not the time to hold personal conversations with one or two audience members while the remainder sit bored.

Do have additional overheads, slides, or PowerPoint displays packed with information about which you did not speak

Way back in chapter 1 of this book, I said that you should only present a subset of your work. This advice still holds. But by doing this, you will necessarily leave yourself open for sharp audience members to identify *apparent* incompleteness in your work. The polite ones will genuinely inquire why you haven't done the work; the unscrupulous ones will attack. Fear not. If you *did* do the work, then you'll be prepared. In cases like this, prepare *ahead of time* additional overheads, slides, or PowerPoint displays packed with the additional information about which you did not speak (see also "The wrong goals" in chapter 1). This may include data, experimental conditions, entire experiments, further assumptions, and so on. You should bring out these overheads, slides, or displays during the question-and-answer period—not during your main presentation, so as not to get off the track of what you came to talk about—in response to audience questions and comments. You will find that this is very powerful. "Good point," you'll say. "I understand exactly what you're saying, and agree with you completely. In fact, I've already addressed that in work I didn't have time to outline in my main presentation. But I do have some additional figures here I can show you that address exactly your point." With this, you will (rightfully) have maintained the upper hand on any criticisms of your work. In fact, the criticisms will ultimately have been unwarranted. Again, as with every other point I've tried to make in this book, having these extra overheads means preparation before you give your presentation, before you face your audience.

Practice your presentation multiple times, out loud, with an overhead, slide, or PowerPoint projector

Okay, you're probably tired of me saying this, but it is really the most important advice I can give you. The amount of practice you have in giving your professional presentation will be directly related to its success or failure. The more practice you have prior to facing your audience, the more prepared overall you will be and the less vulnerable you will be to unwarranted criticisms. So practice your presentation multiple times, out loud, with an overhead, slide, or PowerPoint projector. You may not like it when you're actually doing it, but the first smooth presentation you give in front of an audience will convince you of its importance.

SUMMARY TABLE 3.1 Answering questions and defending your work

Do

- Anticipate questions before your presentation
- Listen to your audience
- Spend time thinking about what the audience says
- Be ready to accept that the audience may be right
- Maintain control over your audience
- Do have additional overheads or slides packed with information
- Practice your presentation multiple times, out loud, with an overhead, slide, or PowerPoint projector

Do not

- Accept impolite audience members
- Accept interruptions
- Invite interruptions

Chapter *4*

Persuasion
On being more influential

On the social psychology of social influence

In this chapter, I outline some of the scientific discoveries made by social psychologists in their study of persuasion and social influence. This chapter will, thus, be very different from the previous three because I will be discussing in some depth various psychological processes and scientific research. I should warn you from the beginning: This is neither an easy chapter to read nor is it one that offers "quick fix" guarantees on being persuasive. There exist no magic incantations nor theatrical gestures that will guarantee your audience will always be persuaded by you. Don't be fooled by public speaking books outlining in simple terms the "10 Ways Guaranteed to Persuade Your Audience." The authors of these books are either uninformed or are lying. Just think about it. People are complex. We are not simple minded automatons. We think, reason, consider, and respond with reference to our personal and socially shared knowledge and values. And because of this, each of the tactics I discuss here will be persuasive under certain circumstances but will fail to be persuasive under others.

We are fortunate, however, because most professional presentations are rather similar to each other in important ways: Their structures are about the same, the audiences will be present for similar reasons (to hear what you have to say!), and your relationship to the audience will be about the same (you'll be there providing information they want to hear). Knowing this will make our task easier by narrowing the range of likely audience responses. Nevertheless, you should still take the information in this chapter as *broad guidelines* for finishing touches *after* you have followed the advice in the previous chapters. And remember, nothing—including the scientific findings in this chapter—will substitute for practice in making a good professional presentation.

The importance of shared group membership

Psychologists—as well as our intuitions—tell us that just as we all are unique individuals, we are all also members of social groups. Not only do we have important differences from other people, but we share important similarities. We have things in common with other people that allow us to cooperate, coordinate, and communicate with each other.[1] Groups allow us to build friendships as well as build cities. And groups provide us with a sense of security and positive self-esteem.[2] These group memberships can be most anything on which people share similarities, including sex, religion, nationality, and ethnicity. Of course, there are many others too; fans of sport teams—even though they are not members of the teams themselves—often become "psychological team members" and refer to the team as "our team," feel good when the team wins, and feel bad when it loses.[3]

So what does this have to do with giving persuasive professional presentations? It has a lot to do with it. An important lesson social psychologists have learned is that *shared group memberships make possible social influence.*[4] It is people in our own group (our "in-group" members) who influence us; people in other groups (our "out-group" members) do not exert social influence upon us. Because of our similarity to fellow in-group members on certain important characteristics we naturally believe that they see and understand the world in the same way we do. In other words, we both come from the same perspective. During times when we are unsure about things, it is our in-group members—people who share our same perspective—that we turn to for understanding. We listen to in-group members, we think about what they have to say, and provided there are the right conditions, we will be persuaded by them.[5] What out-group members say, however, comes from a different perspective and is unlikely to reduce any uncertainty we may have.[6] We are less likely to be persuaded by it.

Presenter influence versus presenter power

As I said above, influence is likely to follow from communications—like those in professional presentations—coming from in-group members. By "influence," I mean actual attitude change, change that has come about upon thoughtful reflection.[7] But aren't there times when we just go along with people, even though we don't really believe them? And aren't there times when we might agree with someone without a lot of thought, but then upon later reflection realize that we actually *disagree*? The answer to both of these questions is yes. For these latter two types of *apparent* persuasion, "power" is a more apt description. Power comes not from in-group members; in-group members don't need to exert power over us because we are receptive to their views, just as they are to our views. It is out-group members—people who are dissimilar to us—who must resort to power tactics in order for us to comply with them.[8] Sometimes these power tactics are coercive, although you hopefully won't be using such tactics in your professional presentations. Other power tactics can be simple tricks that people use to gain short-term compliance. As you will see, the ideas I outline below can take the form of *either* influence or power tactics depending on whether your audience sees you as a fellow in-group member or as an out-group member.

Thinking and nonthinking audiences

In general, the amount of thinking done by your audience will be related directly to how persuaded they are by your presentation. Their amount of thinking will also be related to the persistence of your persuasion; the more people think about what you have to say, the longer-lasting will be any persuasiveness you have.[9] As a presenter, you might find this to be a scary thought because it takes control out of your hands; you, as a presenter, will never have complete control over your audience's thinking. But fear not, opportunities exist.

First, in most professional presentations, audience members are there to listen and learn from you. Most audience members are there to think, otherwise they would not attend at all. Second, but related, is that audience members will listen and think about what you have to say *if they assume you have something of value to say to them*. This will happen *if they see you as a fellow in-group member*. Fortunately, this is very likely in professional presentations. The audience members will be your colleagues; they will be people in *your* profession who share similar beliefs and values about your profession. Of course, there may be audience members who hold different views on the precise content of your work. However, the important group membership in this instance will be that of your profession, and this will provide enough basis to lead your audience members, even the skeptical ones, to listen and think about what you have to say.

Undoubtedly, there will be times when audience members won't listen and think. Sometimes you will be coming to your audience as an "outsider." This might occur, for example, if you are representing one side in a conflict situation. In cases like these, audience members may think you have very little to offer them and may put in little effort considering your ideas. In most professional presentations, however, such conflict situations are less likely to occur. More often than not, nonthinking audience members will be ones who are having a bad day and are preoccupied with other concerns; or they may be people who came to your presentation initially thinking you would talk about something about which they wanted to learn, but who realized that you were actually talking about something different. In these situations, there's not much you can do to increase your audience's attention (but see "What you should do: Tell a story" in chapter 1).

SUMMARY TABLE 4.1 On the social psychology of social influence

- Social influence comes from thinking about communications made by people who are similar to us—people who are in our same social group
- We may comply to power tactics from people who are different from us—people who are in a different social group from us

---

Social influence and power tactics

Because you will encounter some audience members (most, actually) who will think about what you say, and some who won't, it is important for you to recognize and understand the use of both influence and power tactics in your presentation. Here I outline a variety of these, indicating when they take the form of influence and when they take the form of power. In this way, you will be able to use them in the most effective way for your particular presentation situation.

Your similarity to your audience: Be an in-group member

The relative similarity of a presenter to his or her audience is a strong predictor of the ultimate persuasiveness of the communicator—the greater the similarity, the greater the persuasion. This, of course, should come as no surprise, as relative similarity is one of the bases of group membership. And, as I said, social influence emerges from in-group membership; people's attitudes are influenced by others who are relatively similar to themselves on the basis of their group membership.[10] So how do you make sure you are similar to your audience? Again, you don't have to worry too much. When you give a professional presentation, more often than not your audience will be comprised of colleagues and others in your profession. The likelihood is great that the only people attending your presentation will be people similar to you in their profession and in their interest in your topic.

Of course, you can also try to enhance your similarity to your audience. To do this, however, you need to know a little about your audience before you begin. I've said this several times previously, and it remains important here. By knowing who you are talking to, you can adjust yourself and your presentation to fit in better with your audience. You must, however, be careful. It is extremely easy for these attempts to go astray. You can easily come across as disingenuous, which will simply make your audience retreat, turn off, and become resistant to what you have to say.

Your attractiveness and credibility

Similarity and shared group membership lead to attraction.[11] And attractive people are often more persuasive than unattractive people.[12] Although we may initially consider attractiveness as a stable quality, it's easy to realize otherwise. Fashion, for example, changes very quickly, and what we see as fashionable depends on who we identify with and see ourselves as similar to. We may, for example, find crew-cut hair or dreadocks attractive, or we may find suits and ties or multiple facial piercings attractive. For professional presentations, however, this is an easy dilemma to solve. In most cases, professional attire is formal and conservative. If you are unsure, then it is probably best to go with suits and ties, and dresses; your attractiveness to your audience will most likely increase if you are dressed in this manner. Undoubtedly, it does help, again, to know your audience. There may be times when your more conservative clothes will serve only to set you apart from your audience; this will succeed only in making you an out-group member and decreasing your persuasiveness. Again, however, be careful with your attempts to become like in-group members; you may just end up looking foolish.

Your greater credibility, at least in terms of what your audience believes, will also allow you to have greater influence on your audience.[13] And credibility is again related to group membership. Characteristics such as expertise[14] and trustworthiness[15] are more likely to be ascribed to in-group than out-group members. The more you are viewed as a fellow in-group member, the more credibility you will have.

One easy way to make yourself more attractive, credible, and persuasive to your audience is simply by making eye contact with them.[16] In one experimental study, people in the role of job candidates were more likely to be seen as attractive and credible *and* actually to be successful at obtaining their job if they maintained normal to high levels of eye contact with the interviewer.[17] So remember what I said in "Face your audience" in chapter 2 and look at your audience.

The importance of your topic and quality of arguments

The topic you present to your audience and the quality of the arguments that you make are both of utmost importance. It is now clearly known that if your topic is important to your audience members, then the quality of your arguments will be what ends up persuading them.[18] But what makes topics important and arguments good? Obviously, these are both determined by a multitude of factors, some of which will be under your control, and some of which won't. But for professional presentations, there are some guidelines.

In terms of topic importance, most audience members will, again, attend to you precisely because they are interested in what you have to say in the first place. Your audience members will be your colleagues—your in-group members—who share the same perspective and interests that you do. This does not mean that everyone will always be interested in exactly your work. In fact, in "What you should do: Tell a story" in chapter 1 I made a strong case suggesting that your audience would *not* automatically be interested in your work. But recall what I suggested there: Know something about your audience first. By knowing the interests of your audience, you can prepare your presentation in ways that are congruent with their interests. When you do this, you will grab their attention, and they will think about what you're saying.

In terms of argument quality, there are two important things to remember. First, you must always present your work in a clear and logical manner. Chapters 1 and 2 of this book should help you achieve this. However, if you have difficulty with logical construction, then you should consult other sources of help.[19] The second thing to remember is that your arguments are more likely to be *seen* as good *if you are seen as an in-group member to your audience.*[20] This is an interesting bit of social psychology. If you are an in-group member with your audience, not only will your topic be more likely to be of interest to them, but they will find your arguments of better quality. These two things together will help make your talk more influential.

The number and repetition of your arguments

Both the number of arguments you make to support your case and the number of times you say each one are related to how persuasive you will ultimately be. But like everything else, there is not a simple plan. If you have a thinking audience—if your audience sees you as a fellow in-group member who is worthy of listening to—then the more arguments you make the better, *assuming that your arguments are of good quality*. Remember, these are thinking people, and if you just put forward one bad argument after another, they won't be persuaded at all. So more is only better if your arguments are good to begin with. However, if you are, unfortunately, confronted with a nonthinking audience—one that considers you an out-group member—then the argument quality does not actually seem to matter. In this latter case, the research shows that more is simply better.[21]

Does the same hold true for simple repetition of the same argument? Only to a degree. Repeating the same *high-quality* message increases persuasion, but only up to a point. Repeating such a message up to, say, three times seems to be okay. This gives people an opportunity to think about the contents of it. Going beyond three repetitions, however, will simply bore and annoy your audience.[22]

Asking rhetorical questions

Will asking rhetorical questions to your audience make you more persuasive? The answer is maybe. By asking rhetorical questions, you will be explicitly asking your audience to reflect on and think about a specific issue. Under certain circumstances, this could be good. If your audience is already *not* thinking about what you are saying—if your audience, in the first instance, sees what you have to say as relatively unimportant—then asking rhetorical questions will be good, *as long as you have good arguments*. Your rhetorical question will help stimulate your nonthinking audience into thinking. And they will be persuaded by what you have to say as long as your arguments are good. But what if your audience is already thinking? What if you're speaking to an audience that is present to hear what you have to say, an audience that believes already that you have something important to contribute? Hopefully, it is this latter audience you'll be encountering. In this case, rhetorical questions can actually interfere with the thinking that audience members already doing. This would only inhibit your persuasiveness.[23] Given that you will most likely be speaking to audiences that want to be present, you should probably minimize, if not eliminate altogether, your use of rhetorical questions. Of course, if you will knowingly be speaking to an out-group audience, then posing rhetorical questions will help your already-strong arguments.

Stating your position ahead of time and drawing conclusions at the end

In chapter 1, I said that you should start your presentation by stating your objective, the general context, or framework of your work. By following this, you can be confident that your audience will be completely clear about what it is you've come to speak about. But doesn't stating your position from the beginning give a thinking audience a chance to develop counterarguments to your views, thus making you ultimately less persuasive? In some ways, yes. This will be true if you are presenting a view that is opposite to the one held by your audience members on an issue that is important to them *and* if they have the time and ability to think of the alternative views.[24]

So does this mean you should *not* state your objective from the beginning? In general, no. This is for two reasons. First, by stating your objective or general framework at the beginning of your talk you are not necessarily stating your conclusion. That will come later, at a point where you will (hopefully) have provided your audience with sufficient arguments in favor of your view (see "What you should do: Tell a story" in chapter 1). Second, the scientific findings suggest that your audience's resistance will be greater if they have time to think and generate opposing thoughts. But given the pace of a normal presentation, you most likely will not be providing this time for your audience. Of course, your audience could "turn off" and ignore your arguments while they develop their counterviews; over this, you really have no control. The best thing you can do remains presenting your general objective or framework at the beginning. This way, you'll know your message will be the clearest it can be.

What about at the end of your presentation? Should you draw specific conclusions, or would it be more persuasive to let your audience members think through the conclusions for themselves? Well, it's true that if people think an issue is important, *and* if they have time to think about things and draw their own conclusions, then allowing them to do so may allow you to be more persuasive than not.[25] However, in a professional presentation, especially if you have a short amount of time, you will probably have your greatest impact (and certainly leave no room for doubt in your message) if *you* draw the conclusions. In such instances, drawing conclusions yourself will allow you to be more persuasive and more clear.[26]

The speed of your speech

Are fast talkers better persuaders? Like everything else, it depends. Sometimes, faster talkers *are* seen as more credible and are more persuasive.[27] However, fast talkers in professional presentations will not necessarily be the most persuasive. Research has shown that the increased persuasiveness of fast talkers emerges when people have relatively little interest in the issue at hand—as is likely to occur when your audience is comprised of out-group members. But when people *are* interested in the topic, the speed of a communicator's speech does not influence persuasion levels.[28] In fact, there could be instances where the faster pace would actually *inhibit* persuasion in a receptive, thinking audience (an in-group audience). This would occur if the fast pace does not allow your audience actively to listen to and think about what you're saying. So in most professional presentations, you should speak at a moderate pace. If, however, you think you're going to be presenting to an audience with little interest in what you're saying, then an increased speech rate could help your persuasiveness.

Humor: Open with a joke?

Alas, the perennial question, "Should I open with a joke?" The answer yet again is, "It depends." In all cases, you need to ask yourself whether your jokes will be related to the content of your presentation (see "What you should do: Tell a story" in chapter 1). If they're not, don't tell them. Also, you need to determine whether humor is appropriate during your particular professional presentation. Sometimes, humor may be anticipated by your audience and, as such, may be both a necessary component to your successful public speaking and a way of bringing you to the audience—of making you an in-group member.[29] However, your main goal is not to tell jokes. You will not be in front of your audience members as a stand-up comedian, they have come to hear your contributions to your profession. As such, humor may be wholly inappropriate in your professional presentation. As always, you must know your audience.

If a little humor is appropriate, then make sure you are funny. This one I can't help you with, but if you're thinking about it, ask a colleague for an honest opinion. If you're not funny, don't tell jokes. Much of the research on people's moods and their degree of attitude change shows positive moods will, indeed, facilitate persuasion. For an audience that is uninterested in your topic, the people may "misattribute" their positive mood to the message you are providing: "I'm feeling happy. I must, therefore, agree with what this speaker is saying."[30] At the same time, for an audience that *is* interested in the topic—a thinking audience—a positive mood may lead them to generate novel, positive thoughts about the content of what you are saying.[31] But heed my earlier message: If you are not funny, don't do it. Otherwise, all these processes are likely to reverse; you will distance yourself from your audience (decreasing your similarity and credibility), and you may place them in negative moods, leading, ultimately, to greater resistance to your message.

SUMMARY TABLE 4.2 Social influence and power tactics

- Be similar to your audience
- Be attractive and credible
- Ensure your topic is important to your audience and your arguments are good
- More high-quality arguments are better
- Repeat your message up to three times maximum
- Ask rhetorical questions only to out-group audiences
- State your position ahead of time
- Draw conclusions at the end
- Speak at a moderate pace
- Use humor only if it is appropriate *and* if you are funny

Notes

1. Turner, J. C. (1987). A self-categorization theory. In J. C. Turner, M. A. Hogg, P. J. Oakes, S. D. Reicher, & M. S. Wetherell, *Rediscovering the social group: A self-categorization theory* (pp. 42–67). Oxford: Blackwell.
2. Hogg, M. A., & Abrams, D. (1990). Social motivation, self-esteem and social identity. In D. Abrams & M. A. Hogg (Eds.), *Social identity theory: Constructive and critical advances* (pp. 28–47). New York: Springer-Verlag.
3. Branscombe, N. R., & Wann, D. L. (1991). The positive social and self concept consequences of sports team identification. *Journal of Sport and Social Issues, 15,* 115–127.
4. Turner, J. C. (1991). *Social influence.* Buckingham: Open University Press.
5. Mackie, D. M., & Queller, S. (2000). The impact of group membership on persuasion: Revisiting "who said what to whom with what effect?" In D. J. Terry & M. A. Hogg (Eds.). *Attitudes, behavior, and social context: The role of norms and group membership* (pp. 135–155). Mahwah, NJ: Erlbaum; Platow, M. J., Mills, D., & Morrison, D. (2000). The effects of social context, source fairness, and perceived self-source similarity on social influence: A self-categorisation analysis. *European Journal of Social Psychology, 30,* 69–81.
6. McGarty, C., Turner, J. C., Oakes, P. J., & Haslam, S. A. (1993). The creation of uncertainty in the influence process: The roles of stimulus information and disagreement with similar others. *European Journal of Social Psychology, 23,* 17–38.
7. Petty, R. E., & Wegener, D. T. (1998). Attitude change: Multiple roles for persuasion variables. In D. T. Gilbert, S. T. Fiske, & G. Lindzey (Eds.). *The handbook of social psychology* (Vol. 1, 4th ed., pp. 323–390). Boston: McGraw Hill.
8. Turner (1991), op. cit.
9. Petty & Wegener (1998), op. cit.

10. Abrams, D., Wetherell, M. S., Cochrane, S., Hogg, M. A., & Turner, J. C. (1990). Knowing what to think by knowing who you are: Self-categorization and the nature of norm formation, conformity and group polarization. *British Journal of Social Psychology, 29,* 97–119; van Knippenberg, D., & Wilke, H. (1992). Prototypicality of arguments and conformity to ingroup norms. *European Journal of Social Psychology, 22,* 141–155.

11. Byrne, D. (1971). *The attraction paradigm.* New York: Academic Press; Turner (1991), op. cit.

12. Puckett, J. M., Petty, R. E., Cacioppo, J. T., & Fisher, D. L. (1983). The relative impact of age and attractiveness stereotypes on persuasion. *Journal of Gerontology, 38,* 340–343.

13. Petty & Wegener (1998), op. cit.

14. Turner (1987), op. cit.

15. Platow, M. J., McClintock, C. G., & Liebrand, W. B. G. (1990). Predicting intergroup fairness and ingroup bias in the minimal group paradigm. *European Journal of Social Psychology, 20,* 221–239.

16. Edinger, J. A., & Patterson, J. L. (1983). Nonverbal involvement and social control. *Psychological Bulletin, 93,* 30–56.

17. Burgoon, J. K., Manusov, V., Mineo, P., & Hale, J. L. (1985). Effects of gaze on hiring, credibility, attraction and relational message interpretation. *Journal of Nonverbal Behavior, 9,* 133–146.

18. Petty & Wegener (1998), op. cit.

19. See, for example, O'Shea (1999), op. cit.

20. van Knippenberg, D. (1999). Social identity and persuasion: Reconsidering the role of group membership. In D. Abrams & M. A. Hogg (Eds.), *Social identity and social cognition* (pp. 315–331). Oxford: Blackwell Publishers.

21. Petty & Wegener (1998), op. cit.

22. Ibid.

23. Petty, R. E., Cacioppo, J. T., & Heesacker, M. (1981). Effects of rhetorical questions on persuasion: A cognitive response analysis. *Journal of Personality and Social Psychology, 40,* 432–440.

24. Chen, H. C., Reardon, R., Rea, C., & Moore, D. J (1992). Forewarning of content and involvement: Consequences for persuasion and resistance to persuasion. *Journal of Experimental Social Psychology, 28,* 523–541.

25. Stayman, D. M., & Kardes, F. R. (1992). Spontaneous inference processes in advertising: Effects of need for cognition and self-monitoring on inference generation and utilization. *Journal of Consumer Psychology, 1,* 125–142.

26. Petty & Wegener (1998), op. cit.

27. Miller, N., Maruyama, G., Beaber, R. J., & Valone, K. (1976). Speed of speech and persuasion. *Journal of Personality and Social Psychology, 34,* 615–624.

28. Smith, S. M., & Shaffer, D. R. (1995). Speed of speech and persuasion: Evidence for multiple effects. *Personality and Social Psychology Bulletin, 21,* 1051–1060.

29. Bjorklund, D. (1985). Dignified joking: Humor and demeanor in a public speaking club. *Symbolic Interaction, 8,* 33–46.

30. Petty & Wegener (1998), op. cit.

31. Wegener, D. T., Petty, R. E., & Smith, S. M. (1995). Positive mood can increase or decrease message scrutiny: The hedonic contingency view of mood and message processing. *Journal of Personality and Social Psychology, 69,* 5–15.

Chapter 5

Pedagogy
Some comments on teaching students

Classroom lecturing requires the same professionalism as other presentations

In reading through this book, you may have realized that much of my advice for preparing and giving professional presentations can be applied to classroom lecturing as well. This, indeed, is true. This is not to say that good teaching is only good lecturing. Good teaching requires employment of a variety of educational methods and, of course, formal training. My inclusion of this chapter in this book, thus, is not to tell you how to become a good teacher. It is, instead, to remind you that, when you are lecturing to students, you should follow the same principles I have outlined in the first three chapters. High-quality design, delivery, and (yes) defense will yield high-quality lectures.

There are, however, some important differences between giving a professional presentation and lecturing to students, not the least of which are your goals. The goals of lecturing and that of giving professional presentations (see "The right goals" in chapter 1) are *not* the same. When lecturing, your goal is to *educate* students—to pass on knowledge in an area of your expertise to people who do not have this knowledge. As a teacher, your personal contributions to your field and your student ratings (i.e., your impression management) are secondary to your goal of education. When lecturing, education is primary. In addition to differences in goals, you will, of course, encounter a few differences between your professional audiences and your lecture theater of students. Because of these differences in goals and audiences, you'll need to make a few changes in how you give your presentation (i.e., lecture). I outline some of these below.

Designing your lectures

Recognize classroom variability

Your classroom filled with students will almost certainly have a greater variability in ability and prior knowledge than your professional audience. Your professional audience, by simple virtue of audience members being in the profession, will know more and be more homogeneous than your student audience just learning the professional ropes. This variability presents you with more of a challenge. You don't want to bore the highly skilled students, but you don't want to lose the struggling ones. In the end, you'll have to take a stab at some intermediate level, hoping to reach as many students as possible. The very top-end students can remain challenged with the provision of additional reading material, and the very bottom-end students can be coached with special office hours and tutorials. Your goal in your lecture, however, it to reach as many students as possible in one go.

So how do you know what the middle ground is? In the first instance, find out what the prerequisites are for your particular course. What were the books read and other material learned by these students before they came to your class? Knowing this will provide you with a good basis on which to judge their skill level. The second approach is, necessarily, more random: trial and error. At some point you are going to have to face your class and present the material. Give it a go, and see what happens. At the end of your first lecture, ask the students for feedback. Did they understand what you were saying? Where they bored because of the simplistic level? If you are sincere in presenting your questions, the students will see this and give you good feedback. Remember, it is in their best interest to make sure you deliver good lectures.

Relate your lecture material to reading material

Most of the time, you will be asking your students to read some material outside of lectures (often before they arrive to your lectures). It is very important that you relate the content of your lectures to the content of the reading material. This does not mean that you have to lecture word for word out of the reading material. However, there should be some clear connection between lecture and reading. If not, then students will realize this and either become confused or simply stop reading because they see no connection to what you are saying. If there is not a one-to-one connection between the reading and your lecture—and really, there shouldn't be an exact one-to-one connection, or there would be no reason to attend your lecture—then you should outline to students how the readings and lectures are related. Maybe the material in the reading and lectures do not overlap at all except in broad topic. If so, then tell this to the students and explain why you have chosen to run your class in this manner. If, per chance, there is a one-to-one connection between lecture and reading, then tell the students why you've done that (e.g., the reading is particularly difficult, and you explain things better), and why they should continue coming to your lectures.

The fancy stuff may help maintain attention

I still maintain my strong view that the "fancy stuff" should be left out of professional presentations (see "Forget the fancy stuff" in chapter 1). However, when lecturing to a large theater of students, many of whom may not really want to be there in the first place, employing such things as colors, sounds, and videos may help to maintain students' wavering attention. You don't have this problem with professional audiences; they want to be there. But working with students, especially in classrooms of 100, 200, 300, or more people where it is harder to capture each person's attention, then you need to employ what you can. Even a simple switch from overheads to PowerPoint can be quite successful (it was for me!). This, of course, does not mean that you should remove the content of your lectures, nor does it mean that your main job is to be some sort of entertainer. Your main goal remains providing students with information in a clear and meaningful manner. But over the course of, say, a 15-week semester, in which you lecture three times a week, you do run the risk of becoming a boring "talking head." In this instance, employing some of the "fancy stuff" may help maintain students' attention (even though you think that the topics are sufficiently interesting on their own to maintain that attention).

Delivering your lectures

Be aware of the time

It is essential that you arrive to your lectures on time. If you continually arrive late, then students will begin to think (rightly so) that you have no respect for them. This will translate into one simple outcome: a lack of respect for you from the students. When this happens, it will be harder for you to get your message across and harder for you to maintain a quiet lecture theater, the importance of which I discuss later. Moreover, students will begin to arrive late too, which means you may have students wandering into your lecture after you have begun; this is very distracting for you and the other students.

Not only should you arrive on time, but you should end your lectures on time too. Going overtime, of course, annoys students and may make them late for their next class. Ending early, however, also can be problematic. Of course, ending one or two lectures early will be well greeted by students. However, continually ending lectures early will yield two negative outcomes. First, students will get in the habit of leaving early and will start packing up their books and writing material before the scheduled end of your lecture. If you are *not* finished with your lecture, you (and other students) will find this noise to be quite disconcerting and distracting. Second, if you continually end your lectures early, some students will become angry at continually being shortchanged. They have come to your lectures expecting a certain amount of information in a specified period of time. When you don't provide it, you'll be cheating them.

Speak at a note-taking pace

When you are lecturing to students, remember that they are also writing down what you say. Because of this, you will have to speak at a much slower pace than you would in a professional presentation. In fact, it is a good idea to repeat everything you say at least once, if not twice. By doing this, you may find that you'll get a reputation of repeating yourself (as I do!), but you'll also find that students will actually be grateful for the chance to write down what you say (as my students tell me in their written evaluations). When you are just beginning, of course, you may not know precisely what pace you should take. Again, simply ask the students. If they tell you that you're going too fast, then slow down.

Maintain quiet in the lecture theater

When speaking to professional audiences, you can be sure that they are attending your presentation because they want to hear what you have to say. Unfortunately, this is not always true with students. Sometimes you'll be teaching a class that students are taking only because it is required. Sometimes students will be genuinely interested in your topic, but the sunshine outside will be even more enticing. Whatever the reason, students may become antsy and start talking to each other. This can become a disaster for you and the remainder of the students if it gets out of hand. Make sure you maintain quiet in your lecture theater. There are a variety of ways of doing this, each of which you'll have to try out on your own. But here are a couple of suggestions. When students start talking, you should simply stop. Because students expect you always to speak, they should notice when you're not and attend to you (to see what's wrong, perhaps) instead of their neighbor. If that doesn't work, simply tell the class to be quiet. If that's not enough, you can begin with the threats; the first is to remind students that they are responsible for the material whether they are paying attention or not; the second is that you'll ask noisy students to leave; and the third is that you, yourself, will leave. Of course, none of these are guarantees, so you'll have to see what works best for you and your particular cohort of students.

You may want to encourage questions

Part of my advice to you in chapter 3 was not to invite questions from your audience during the presentation itself when presenting to professional audiences. When lecturing to students, however, inviting questions may be an important part of the learning process. Your goal when lecturing is not to get through the lecture you prepared for that day; it is, instead, to ensure the students have learned. If they haven't, you'll have done your job poorly. So inviting students to ask questions—both for clarification and for extrapolation—can be a valuable part of the teaching process. And like giving professional presentations, make sure you repeat the question asked to you to ensure that you understand it and so that the rest of the class can hear it. Of course, you'll have to ensure that your lecture session does not simply turn into an open discussion (unless that's your goal). In the end, you did prepare your lecture under the assumption that its content was appropriate for the students to learn. It is completely reasonable for you to limit the number of questions asked by students to give you a chance to provide the education you intended.

Defending your lectures

You know more than the students
(but it's okay to admit not knowing)

A source of anxiety for many people lecturing is that the students will ask questions for which they, the lecturers, do not know the answer. The fear of not knowing enough, and not knowing all the answers to all the questions, is a common source of anxiety for lecturers. Fear not, however. Remember, you are the teacher, not the student. You achieved your position *because* you know a lot. Almost invariably, you will know more about the topic on which you are lecturing than the students will know. Because of this, you will be able to answer most if not all questions posed to you. If, however, a question is posed for which you do not know the answer, pause and think about it for a minute, as recommended in "Spend time thinking about what the audience says" in chapter 3. Sometimes you will not know the answer because the question itself does not make sense. If so, ask for clarification. Sometimes you will not know the answer because the question is on a topic other than one pertinent to the class (and, hence, your expertise). If so, explain this to the student and invite the student to meet with you after the class if he or she is keen to pursue the issue. And sometimes, the question is a good one on the appropriate topic, but you will simply not know the answer. That's okay. You can't know every possible piece of knowledge, even in your area of expertise. If this happens, say something like, "Hmm, that's a very good question. I actually don't know the answer to that, but I'll make sure to look it up and tell you the answer during the next lecture." Students will typically be very receptive to this type of comment and will neither think you are incapable nor that you have just brushed them aside. Make sure, however, that you do look up the answer and that you do report it during the next lecture!

SUMMARY TABLE 5.1 Some comments on teaching

- Your goal as a teacher is to educate
- Recognize classroom variability and choose an academic level to suit as many students as possible
- Relate your lecture material to the reading material
- The fancy stuff may help maintain attention
- Be aware of the time
- Speak at a note-taking pace
- Maintain quiet in the lecture theater
- You may want to encourage questions
- You know more than the students (but it's okay to admit not knowing)

Chapter **6**

Prototypes
Examples of good and bad overheads and slides

Looking at some examples

In the few pages of this final chapter, I provide you with some simple examples of good and bad overheads and slides (including PowerPoint slides). Each of the pages is written as a separate overhead or slide. I have annotated various points with callout shapes indicating where in the book you can learn why it is a good or bad feature. Of course, your own overheads and slides will vary from these given your own professional content; however, these examples include several of the points I've made in Chapter 1. Note that the font sizes as they appear on the overhead examples and PowerPoint slides are not the appropriate sizes because they had to be altered to fit onto the book pages. Also note that because the pages of this book are smaller than your overheads will be, you will have more room than I had for my examples. Finally, it is worth saying that a simple glance through these examples without reading at least the first three chapters will not prepare you adequately for giving successful professional presentations; these examples are supplementary to the core of what I have said.

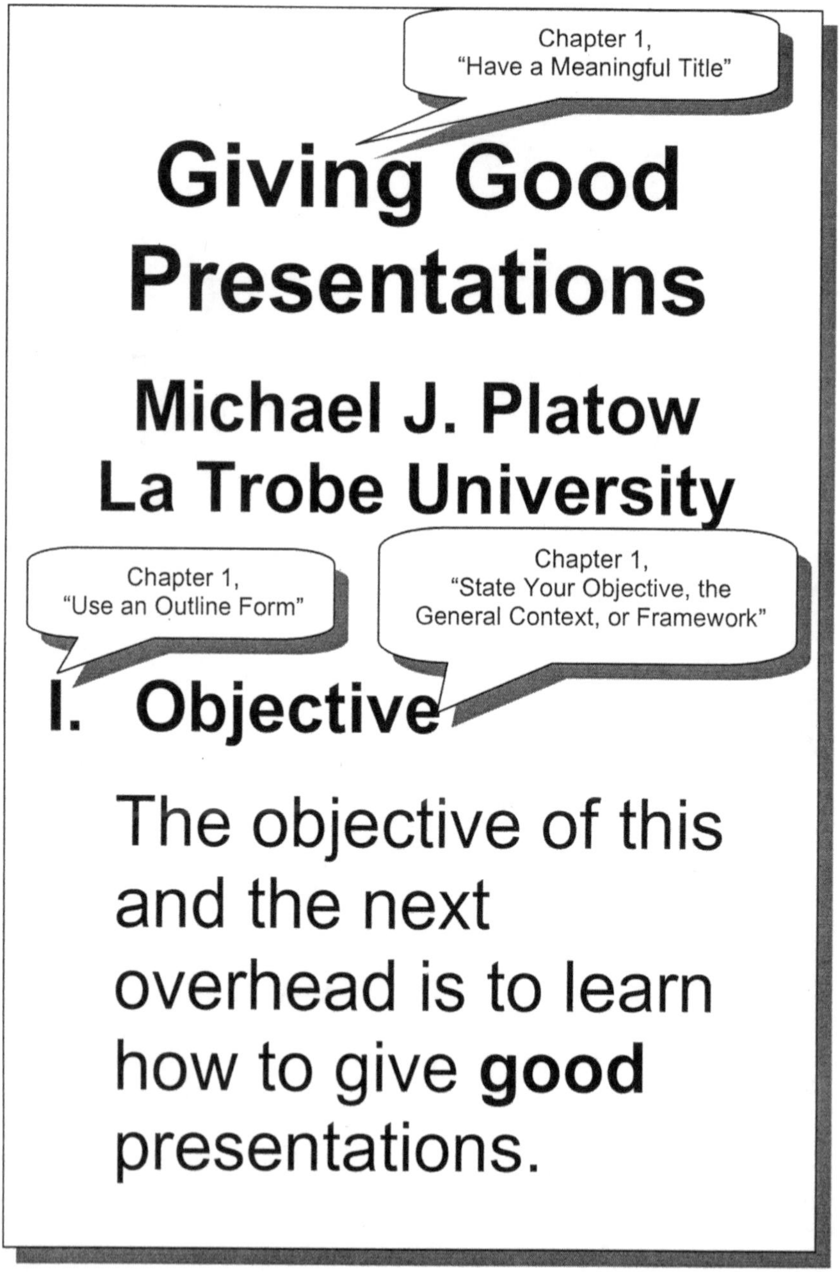

FIGURE 6.1 An example of good overheads.

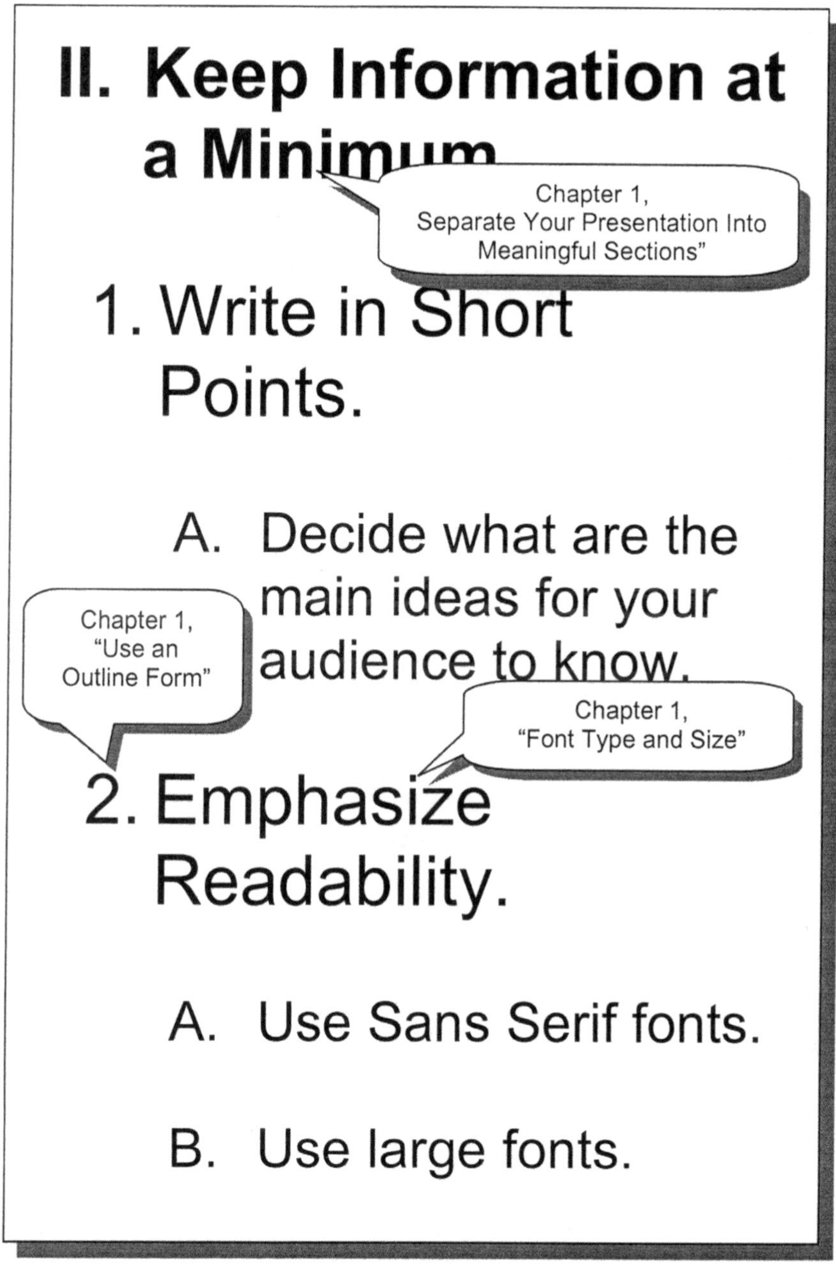

II. Keep Information at a Minimum

> Chapter 1,
> Separate Your Presentation Into
> Meaningful Sections"

1. Write in Short Points.

> Chapter 1,
> "Use an
> Outline Form"

A. Decide what are the main ideas for your audience to know.

> Chapter 1,
> "Font Type and Size"

2. Emphasize Readability.

A. Use Sans Serif fonts.

B. Use large fonts.

FIGURE 6.1 (continued).

Giving Bad Presentations
Michael J. Platow
La Trobe University

Chapter 1,
"Font Type and Font Size:

My goal in writing this slide is to demonstrate how *not* to write your overheads.

If you want to give a bad talk, don't bother watching the time!

Chapter 1,
"Forget the Fancy Stuff"

Chapter 1,
"Separate Your Presentation Into Meaningful Sections"

One *sure way* to confuse your **audience** is to emphasize so many WORDS in each sentence that your **audience** doesn't know what to attend to.

Chapter 1,
"Do Not Include Names and Dates"

Turner (1991) argues that we are influenced by ingroup members, not outgroup members.

---One big mistake people often make is to clutter their overheads and slides by placing too much information on them. You should avoid this in at least two ways if you want to give a good talk:
    *Always use double-spacing   and
    *If you want to emphasize a point,
you should bold it rather than using italics or underlining.

Chapter 1,
"Readability: Spacing, Emphasis, and Printing"

FIGURE 6.2 An example of a bad overhead.

Writing Good Slides and PowerPoint Displays

1. When making slides and PowerPoint displays, remember:

Chapter 1, "Working with PowerPoint

A. Don't get carried away with colour.
   i. Pale blue and pink backgrounds are OK.
   ii. Saturated blue and red text is OK.

B. Animation and canned sounds are annoying.

C. Follow the rules for good overheads to make good slides and PowerPoint displays.

Chapter 1, "Making Overheads and Slides"

FIGURE 6.3 An example of a good slide.

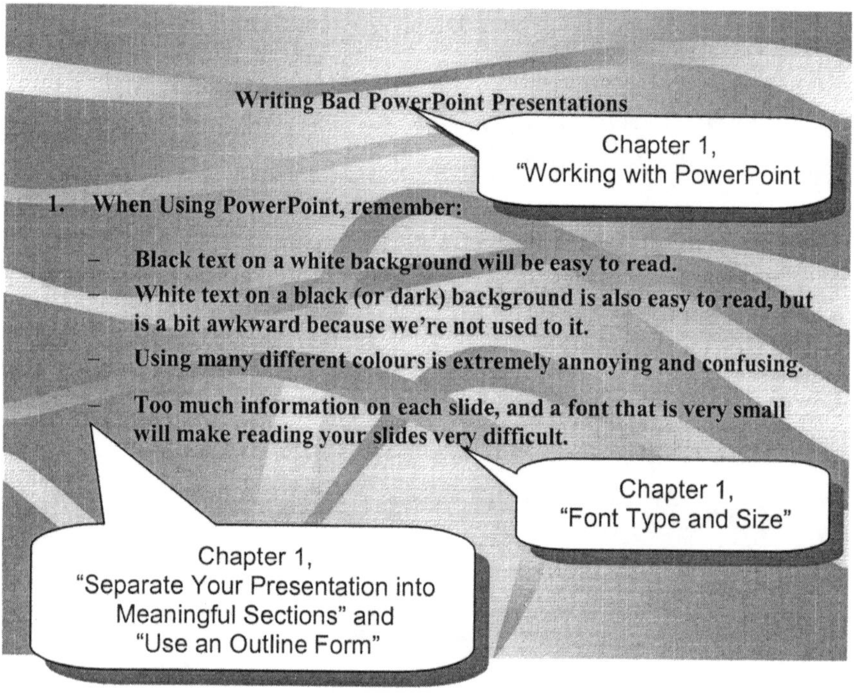

FIGURE 6.4 An example of a bad slide.

Index

animation. *See* visual aids animation; graphs animation
anxiety, ix, 1, 34, 35, 38, 40, 47, 73
arguments, 17,63,64
  number of, 62, 63
  quality of, 62
  repetition of, 62, 63
arrival, x, 41
attractiveness, 61
audience
  attention of, 6, 8, 9, 25, 31, 34-37, 39, 41, 42, 43, 59, 60, 71, 72
  expectations, 5, 10, 18, 29, 30, 32, 41, 43, 65, 72, 73
  comments, 50-55
  comprehension, 2, 3, 5, 10, 14, 15, 17, 24, 28-31, 34, 39–42, 44, 45, 58, 64, 70, 71, 73
  confusion. *See* audience, comprehension
  control, 47, 52, 53, 59
  criticism, 10
  facing your audience, 35–37, 62
  in-group/out-group, 59-65
  interest, 5, 6, 8, 9, 12, 44, 62, 63, 65

interruptions, 47, 53, 54
knowing your audience, 6, 9, 18, 49, 50, 61, 62, 65
meeting your audience, 45
noise. *See* audience, quiet
(non)thinking, 59, 60, 62–65
questions, x, 1 , 5, 10, 15, 34, 35, 40, 47, 49–53, 55, 73
quiet, 37, 38, 41, 72, 73
rude, x, 47, 51, 53, 54
similarity. *See* audience, in-group/ out-group
(un)sophistication, 9, 44
variability, 70

charts. *See* graphs
conclusions, 14, 54, 63, 64
contributions, 2, 5, 9, 18, 40, 44, 45, 63, 65, 70
credibility, 15, 61, 64, 65
cutting, 5, 9, 10, 12, 46, 47

defending your work, 47, 49–56, 69, 73
delivery, x, 33–48, 69, 71
design, x, 1–32, 69, 70